THE
IL FORNAIO

PASTA BOOK

# THE IL FORNAIO

# Pasta Book

*Authentic Recipes Celebrating Italy's Regional Pasta Dishes*

*by*

## MAURIZIO MAZZON

*photographs*
*by*
*Michael Lamotte*

**CHRONICLE BOOKS**
SAN FRANCISCO

Library of Congress
Cataloging-in-Publication Data:

Mazzon, Maurizio.

The Il Fornaio pasta book :
authentic recipes celebrating
Italy's regional pasta dishes /
by Maurizio Mazzon.

p. cm.
Includes index.
ISBN 0-8118-3016-0
1. Cookery (Pasta)
2. Cookery, Italian. I. Title.

TX809.M17 M373 2002
641.8'22—dc21

2001053702

Manufactured in China

Prop styling by Sara Slavin
Food styling by Sandra Cook
Designed by Michael Mabry

Photographer Michael Lamotte
wishes to thank Sara Slavin,
Sandra Cook, Carol Rossi,
Hilary Wolf, and Gail Lamotte
for making this experience so
enjoyable.

Distributed in Canada by
Raincoast Books
9050 Shaughnessy Street
Vancouver, BC V6P 6E5

10 9 8 7 6 5 4 3 2

Chronicle Books LLC
85 Second Street
San Francisco, California 94105

www.chroniclebooks.com

INTRODUCTION 6

IN THE KITCHEN AND AT THE TABLE 8

PASTA GLOSSARY 10

INGREDIENTS 17

EQUIPMENT 19

CLASSIC RECIPES 21

TECHNIQUES FOR COOKING PERFECT PASTA 26

HOW TO SERVE PASTA 27

*At the Top of the Boot* 29

LIGURIA 34

PIEMONTE E VAL D'AOSTA 39

LOMBARDIA 47

TRENTINO-ALTO ADIGE 54

FRIULI-VENEZIA GIULIA 62

VENETO 66

*In the Heartland* 79

EMILIA-ROMAGNA 85

TOSCANA 93

UMBRIA 100

MARCHE 105

LAZIO 107

ABRUZZO E MOLISE 115

*Along the Southern Shoreline* 119

CAMPANIA 124

BASILICATA 135

CALABRIA 138

PUGLIA 139

*On the Islands* 145

SARDEGNA 151

SICILIA 156

SOURCES 170

MAURIZIO MAZZON'S FAVORITE ITALIAN PROVERBS 171

ACKNOWLEDGMENTS 172

INDEX 173

TABLE OF EQUIVALENTS 180

Italians are passionate. We do everything with great energy. When we speak, we wave our hands enthusiastically in the air. When we meet friends and family, we embrace as though it is for the first and last time. And when we sit down for a meal, well, we eat with a powerful gusto that cannot be rivaled.

Food is not just sustenance for us. It is our history, our culture, and our provincial legacy. For us, food is so much more than a meal. It is a pastime, an art, and a lifelong love affair. We love to eat—it nourishes our souls and feeds our hearts. The only delight greater than indulging in the pleasures of the table is sharing them. That desire—to introduce others to authentic Italian cuisine—is the reason I have written this book.

For me, the food that is the most Italian is pasta. It is the cornerstone of our diet. Universally prepared, consumed, and loved, pasta is, undeniably, a uniquely democratic food that crosses geographical borders, religious differences, and socioeconomic divides. Its cultural worth is as vast as its enormous variety of shapes and sizes. As long as there is wheat and water, pasta will be made, and it will fill the stomachs of the rich and the poor, the young and the old, the native Italians, and the Italians at heart.

The Etruscans—one of Italy's earliest civilizations—were the first Italian residents to prepare pasta. Tools have been found in the caves where these Tuscan dwellers lived during the first thousand years B.C. that were used to sculpt the simple mixture of wheat and water into rudimentary shapes not unlike some of the pasta available today. Romans, whose civilization followed the Etruscans', ate mostly grain. They increased the popularity of pasta during their reign, spreading its reach throughout the country, and eventually, the world.

As the scope of pasta's dietary dominance grew, it developed regional distinctions within Italy. Fresh pasta made with refined flours began to appear in the north by the fourteenth century. It was adorned with savory cream and cheese sauces due to the abundance of these ingredients. In the south, pasta was predominately made from the semolina flour grown in the area and was enhanced with sun-ripened tomatoes, fresh vegetables, and fruity olive oils.

In Italy, our regional identity is very strong—it can be likened to the way Californians, Texans, and other Americans identify as much with their home state as with the nation. We are not so much Italian as we are Venetian, Sicilian, or Umbrian, and our regional loyalty is expressed in our local cuisine.

Growing up in Marcon, a small town near Venice in the Veneto region, I was raised on pasta dishes prepared by my mother that featured ingredients from the region's bounty—lots of seafood, spices, and local produce. Venice is where I learned to cook and where my love for the authentic dishes of Italy and its regions was ignited. It is my mission to preserve the regional dishes that

compose the culinary landscape of Veneto as well as the other regions of Italy. To let them fade from the kitchen or the table would be to ignore the breadth and depth of Italian culture.

At Il Fornaio we believe that bringing these regional traditions to America is extremely important. To do so, we showcase the diversity of Italy's twenty regions with our Festa Regionale—a two-week celebration every month that features a regional dinner menu. Every menu includes pasta, main courses, bread, wine, and dessert from the selected region. To ensure the authenticity of the menus, each year I travel with nine or ten of my chefs to Italy. We visit five to six regions, eating at new and old favorite restaurants, touring the markets, and meeting with food purveyors. It rejuvenates and inspires us.

I tasted many of the recipes in this book for the first time on one of my Chef's Tours. Others I learned during my years of cooking in Venice, and some were taught to me by the talented chefs whom I've worked with over the years. These are the dishes that I love to cook over and over again in my own kitchen with ingredients I purchase in the markets near my home in California.

This collection of my favorite pasta dishes, culled from all twenty regions of Italy, will give you an opportunity to experience the most authentic Italian cuisine outside of Italy. These home-style recipes will be easy to prepare in your kitchen and will delight the friends and family at your table. I hope that you will have the pleasure to prepare and partake of every recipe. Buon appetito!

—Maurizio Mazzon

To be a chef is to know how to peel an asparagus spear, scrub a pot, and clean a squid. A chef understands that what is placed on a plate is linked to every action, every ingredient, and every utensil that makes up the whole of a kitchen. You can learn to cook from a book, but it is practice and experience that will lead you to become a chef.

When I was still a teenager, I entered the kitchen of a chef with nearly fifty years more cooking experience than I had. He gave me menial tasks to perform. I wondered when I would be able to cook with the same skill and confidence as this chef and others whom I admired so much.

It wasn't until I learned the relationship between cleaning the burnt remains out of a soiled pot and knowing how to prevent it that I took my place at the stove. When rolling gnocchi with my palms became as familiar as clapping my hands together, I was taught how to cook the savory dumplings. When a knife began to feel like an extension of my arm, the weight of a pan held at arm's length was no longer noticeable, and the heat of the grill beckoned rather than repelled, I began my journey to become a chef. In Italy, first you learn to shell a pea, then you learn to cook it.

If you want to master the preparation of pasta, first you must understand the different types of pasta, how to select the best ingredients, and how to prepare the recipes that are the foundation for so many pasta dishes.

Pasta is perhaps the greatest expression of Italian artistry. Flour, water, and a few other basic ingredients are transformed into an endless selection of shapes and sizes.

Although fresh and dry pasta are considered the same food, no foods that share the same name could be more different. To me they are like sneakers for men and stiletto heels for women: both can be called shoes, serve the same purpose, and are made from similar materials, but you cannot confuse the two.

To help you select the perfect pasta and understand its best qualities, I have listed and described all of the forms of pasta that appear in this book. Fresh and dry pasta are listed separately. Some types of pasta are available both ways, and for the purposes of this book, I have included most of them with the fresh pasta. In some cases, for convenience, dry pasta may be substituted for fresh.

*When it's prepared correctly, eating fresh pasta is an ethereal culinary experience. Make it at home if you can, or purchase a reputable brand at your local market. Packaged fresh pasta rarely tastes the same as homemade. Although it may take more time to prepare, the satisfaction derived from eating pasta that you made by hand makes it taste all the more delicious.*

*Fresh pasta primarily comprises flour, eggs, and other dairy products, such as milk, ricotta, and grated cheese. Its ingredients give it a soft texture and absorbent surface. It is cut or formed into a variety of shapes, including sheets used to enclose a filling.*

## Dumplings

**CANEDERLI** (kah-NEH-dehr-lee). Sometimes referred to as gnocchi, canederli originated in northern Italy and are similar to a matzo ball in texture and serving style. Made with bread instead of flour, they can include a wide range of ingredients, such as vegetables or cheese.

**GNOCCHI** (n'YOH-kee). These light and savory dumplings are prepared all over Italy. Generally, gnocchi made with potato, all-purpose flour, and eggs are popular in the north, and those made with semolina (from durum flour) are favored in the south. Additionally, gnocchi can include vegetables and dairy products. Packaged gnocchi are poor substitutes for fresh, but are acceptable if you don't have time to make them. Gnocchetti are a smaller version of gnocchi. Don't confuse dry pasta labeled "gnocchi" with fresh dumplings.

**MALLOREDDUS** (mah-loh-REH-duce). A southern style of gnocchi prepared with semolina flour. In Sardegna they are further enhanced with the addition of saffron.

**SPÄTZLE** (SH'PEHT-z'l). Originally from Germany, these savory, oblong dumplings are popular in Alto Adige. Like pasta, they can be prepared with many different ingredients, such as spinach or bread crumbs and nutmeg.

## Round Strands

**PICI** (PEE-chee). These twisted Tuscan noodles are medium length—about 6 inches long—and are thicker than spaghetti.

## Ribbons

**CHITARRINE** (kee-tah-REE-neh). This noodle was created in Abruzzo and is named for the tool used to cut the dough, the *chitarra*, which produces thin, flat strands.

**FETTUCCINE** (feh-too-CHEE-neh). This slightly broad noodle consists of flour and egg and often a wide variety of ingredients, including spinach, lemon, and black pepper. Dry fettuccine can be substituted for fresh.

**TAGLIATELLE** (tah-l'yah-TEH-leh). A long, flat pasta that looks like ribbons. It is slightly wider than taglierini and tagliolini, which, in descending order, differ by mere millimeters in width. Their names come from the word *tagliare*, "to cut," and are popular in the north. Dry tagliatelle is available in packages and can be substituted for fresh.

## Stuffed Pastas

**BOCCON** (boh-KOHN). A Veneto style of gnocchi typically made with ricotta cheese and spinach mixed in the dough. The name translates as "bite-size."

**CANNELLONI** (kah-neh-LOH-nee). Literally translated, *cannelloni* means "big tubes." This fresh pasta is rolled around a savory filling and is usually baked casserole style.

**CAPPELLACCI** (kah-peh-LAH-chee). Pasta from Emilia-Romagna named for their shape—"small hats." The pasta dough for the classic squash-filled cappellacci is made with flour and squash.

**CASONSEI** (kah-sohn-SAY). Stuffed pastas from Lombardia and Veneto. Traditionally shaped as horseshoes or half moons, they are often prepared with flavored pasta, such as beet pasta.

**CULURGIONIS** (koo-lur-JOH-nehs). From Sardegna, these ravioli are traditionally stuffed with a pecorino cheese and vegetable filling. Just as the filling varies from town to town, so does the spelling and pronunciation of its name.

**LASAGNE** (lah-ZAH-n'yeh). A large sheet of pasta typically layered alternately with a sauce and baked. Dry lasagne noodles are available in a variety of widths. They should be at least 5 inches long if you want to substitute them for a large fresh sheet.

**OFELLE** (oh-FEH-leh). A Friuli specialty, this type of square ravioli is made from a potato pasta and is stuffed with a savory filling.

**PANSOTI** (pahn-SOH-tee). These ravioli are a Liguria specialty. From the dialect word of the region, *pansa*, meaning "belly."

**RAVIOLI** (rah-vee-OH-lee). Almost all stuffed pasta falls under the label of ravioli. Region by region the name and filling changes, as is apparent in the following types of ravioli included in this book. Typically prepared with a basic pasta dough of flour and eggs, ravioli may include a variety of ingredients, from potatoes to beets.

## Tubes

**GARGANELLI** (gahr-gah-NEH-lee). This fresh pasta, found primarily in Emilia-Romagna, starts as a square. It is then rolled around a dowel and over a small comb-like tool to extract its final shape and texture, which is a grooved, diamond-shaped tube.

## Wide, Flat Noodles

**CRESPELLE** (kreh-SPEH-leh). These thin, delicate pancakes may seem out of place in a lineup of pasta, but they are prepared with the same ingredients—flour, eggs, and milk—illustrating the diversity of pasta.

**FAZZOLETTI** (fah-tzoh-LEH-tee). This pasta is named for its triangular, handkerchief shape.

**PAPPARDELLE** (pah-pahr-DEH-leh). This pasta, a favorite of Tuscans, is a wide ribbon about 1 inch wide and 8 to 9 inches long. Dry pappardelle can be used in recipes that call for fresh.

**PIZZOCCHERI** (pee-TZOH-keh-ree). These fresh noodles from Lombardia, made with buckwheat flour and milk, are ½ inch wide and 4 to 5 inches long.

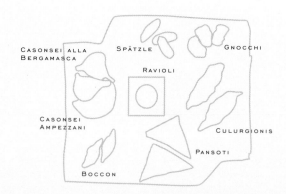

*Dry pasta has its virtues. When cooked perfectly* al dente, *"firm to the bite," its hearty, toothsome texture is gratifying. It is a staple throughout Italy and most popular in the south. It is also a convenient substitute for the fresh pasta called for in many of the recipes in this book.*

*Dry pasta comprises mostly semolina—flour made from durum wheat—and water. It is less absorbent than fresh pasta, which makes it ideal for matching with olive oil and tomato-based sauces. The best dry pasta is uniform in color and has a slightly rough texture to help grab the sauce.*

---

### Round Strands

BIGOLI (BEE-goh-lee). The true noodle of Veneto, bigoli was originally prepared with buckwheat flour and formed with a special pasta maker called the *bigolaro.* They were long noodles with hollow centers, but today bigoli are solid, round noodles made primarily from whole-wheat flour.

BUCATINI (boo-kah-TEE-nee). Long strands that are hollow in the center.

PERCIATELLI (pehr-ch'yah-TEH-lee). A little larger than bucatini, perciatelli are also long and hollow in the center.

SPAGHETTI (spah-GEH-tee). These long, round noodles are one of the most beloved types of pasta used in Italian cookery. Spaghettini and vermicelli are thinner versions of this very popular pasta.

### Ribbons

LINGUINE (leen-GWEE-neh). Shaped like flat ribbons, linguine are much thinner versions of fettuccine (see "Fresh Pasta").

TRENETTE (treh-NEH-teh). Nearly identical to linguine, trenette is from Liguria. Typically, it is served with a pesto sauce.

## Shapes

CAVATAPPI (kah-vah-TAH-pee). Each thick, round strand of pasta is twisted into a corkscrew shape; cavatappi are very popular in the southern regions.

CAVATELLI (kah-vah-TEH-lee). Derived from the word *cavare*, "to hollow out," this pasta looks like a tiny, ridged square that has curled up.

CONCHIGLIE (kohn-CHEE-l'yeh). A shell-shaped pasta that is ideal for cradling chunky sauces.

FARFALLE (fahr-FAH-leh). Often called butterfly or bow-tie pasta, these noodles are about 2 inches long and make heavenly pillows for creamy sauces.

FUSILLI (foo-SEE-lee). Short, compact, corkscrew-shaped pasta paired with sauces containing chopped ingredients, which are caught in the grooves of the pasta.

GEMELLI (jeh-MEH-lee). This pasta's name translates as "twins." Although it looks like two identical strands twisted together (hence the name), it is actually one round strand folded in half and twisted.

ORECCHIETTE (oh-reh-K'YEH-teh). Called "little ears," this pasta from Puglia is shaped by forming it into little circles and indenting them in the center.

## Short Tubes

PENNE (PEH-neh). This pasta is shaped like a quill, from which its name is derived. (*Penna* is Latin for "quill.") The short, hollow noodles are cut on the diagonal. Pennette is a smaller version. Penne rigate are ribbed; penne lisce are smooth.

RIGATONI (ree-gah-TOH-nee). Larger than penne, rigatoni are short, fat tubes named for their ridged texture. (*Riga* is Italian for "ridge.")

TORTIGLIONI (tohr-tee L'YOH-nee). Short, fat tubes with spiral grooves on their surfaces.

## INGREDIENTS

*The Italian pantry is neither fancy nor complicated. It consists of flavorful, high-quality ingredients, which, when combined with simple techniques, result in one of the world's most flavorful cuisines.*

*There are two general rules to follow for stocking a pantry. First, don't cut corners, or you will jeopardize the integrity of the dish. And second, when fresh is available, use it in place of canned or frozen. With that said, I'd like to offer further advice about the ingredients that you will need to prepare the recipes in this book.*

BASIL. Fresh basil is a fragile leaf that should be torn, not cut. Be sure to buy and use basil when it is dark green, and free of brown edges or wilted leaves. Wash basil by rinsing it under cold running water, and then set it on a towel to air-dry.

BREAD CRUMBS. The best bread crumbs are those you make yourself. You can use almost any type, but breads with added ingredients such as olives, nuts, or seeds may give your dish an unwanted flavor. Chop fresh or slightly stale bread in the bowl of a food processor until a fine crumb is achieved. Use the crumbs fresh, or dry in a low-temperature oven; store in an airtight container.

BUTTER. Use only unsalted butter for cooking. This allows you to control the level of salt in any dish.

EGGS. Large eggs are specified for the recipes in this book. Using smaller or larger eggs may affect the quality of the dish, especially the fresh pasta recipes.

GARLIC. Much of the flavor of garlic is from its oil. To release the oil, peel the cloves and, using the blade of a knife, press down on it to smash it. Use the clove as is or, if necessary, chop it briefly after it is smashed. If a green sprout has grown, cut the clove in half and remove it.

GRANA. In Italy the generic term used for grated hard cheeses is *grana*. Many of the recipes in this book call for grated cheese as an ingredient or finish. The two used primarily are Parmigiano-Reggiano, a cow's milk cheese, and pecorino, a sheep's milk cheese. There is only one Parmigiano-Reggiano; it is made in Emilia-Romagna. Nearly every region makes a version of pecorino. Veneto and Lombardia are home to grana padano—a hard cheese made from cow's milk that is similar to Parmigiano-Reggiano. Whichever cheese you use should be freshly grated. There is no substitute.

HERBS. I use only fresh herbs in my recipes. I do not own any dried herbs; to me, they cannot compare in flavor to fresh herbs. I strongly suggest that you begin an herb garden if you don't already have one. Rosemary, sage, and basil are simple to grow and are great to have on hand.

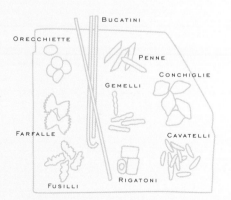

Olive
There a
extra-vi
pressed
acidity,
and ver
restaura
a condi
oil from
"Pure"
pressing
cooking

Dry p
pasta w
Check t
broken
or Rust

Dried
Italy is
spices.
slender,
water i

Grou
taste th
per, wit
taste of
stove fo
freshly
half to
the pap
uring s

Sea s
Harvest
salt is n
or "fine
Keep a
recipes

For most Italians, making fresh pasta is second nature. For others it takes a little practice before it becomes effortless. I began when I was just a small boy. My mother would ask me to turn the handle of the pasta maker, and although my arm would grow tired, I did not stop because I wanted to prove I was strong. The best advice that I can give anyone is to have fun. Additionally, use your hands. How the dough feels—its progression from a crumbly mixture to soft, pliable pasta dough—is the best indication of how long it should be kneaded to ensure that it will roll out beautifully.

## BASIC PASTA

1 ¼ cups all-purpose flour

½ teaspoon sea salt

2 large eggs at room temperature

1 teaspoon olive oil

Note: Humidity can affect the moisture level of pasta dough. If a dough is too moist, add flour as you knead it. Conversely, if it is too dry, add a small amount of water. Judging how dough should feel becomes more comfortable with practice, so don't be discouraged if it takes a few times before you learn to make perfect pasta.

## STEP-BY-STEP GUIDE FOR MAKING PASTA

1. In a large shallow bowl or on a flat work surface, shape the dry ingredients into a mound. Make a well in the center.

2. Place the liquid ingredients in the well and beat with a fork, gradually beating in a wider path and incorporating the flour in very small amounts.

3. Continue mixing with the fork until the dough begins to resemble a dry, crumbly mixture.

4. Transfer to a flour-dusted, flat work surface and begin kneading by hand: Roll the dough sideways across the surface, from hand to hand, applying strong pressure while squeezing the dough. Knead until all of the flour is incorporated, no floury white spots remain, and the dough begins to soften and is no longer sticky, 3 to 5 minutes.

5. Shape into a ball, cover with plastic wrap, and let sit 30 minutes. (This allows the flour to continue to absorb moisture from the eggs.)

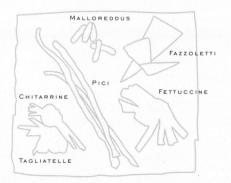

MALLOREDDUS

FAZZOLETTI

PICI

CHITARRINE

FETTUCCINE

TAGLIATELLE

## To Roll Out Strands and Ribbons:

1. Adjust the pasta maker to its widest setting. Dust the surface next to the pasta maker with flour.

2. Cut the dough into 2 portions.

3. Working with one portion at a time, shape the dough into a flat disk. Flatten one edge further to fit between the rollers. Feed the dough into the rollers and begin rolling out the dough, stretching it as you feed it into the pasta maker.

4. Sprinkle lightly with flour, then fold in thirds and roll it through again, pulling the dough taut to stretch it as it goes through the rollers. Repeat 12 to 14 times, each time folding the dough in half before rolling it out.

5. Adjust the pasta maker to the next setting, fold the dough in half, and roll out once. Repeat this procedure on the middle setting, gently stretching the dough as it is fed into the rollers. Dust with flour. The pasta should be the same width as the rollers.

6. Roll out the dough on the last setting to form a sheet the same width as the pasta maker, 48 inches long, and 1/16 inch thick. Roll out the second piece of dough in the same manner.

7. Cut the dough into the length indicated in the recipe. To cut into noodles: Gently feed one sheet into the pasta maker cutting attachment while turning the handle at a consistent speed. Or, cut the pasta into the width indicated using a very sharp knife or pastry cutter.

## To Dry Strands and Ribbons:

Hang the strands on a rack or arrange in loose coils and set on a flour-dusted plate, as directed in the recipe. If you don't have a rack, you can rest a rolling pin between two chairs and hang the pasta over it or lay the pasta flat on the counter and dust with flour. Most pasta will dry sufficiently within 2 hours. If you have one, a small fan will help to dry the pasta. If you want to dry it longer, it can sit for up to 24 hours. Move the pasta 2 or 3 times to prevent it from sticking together. Never put damp pasta in a plastic bag or sealed container.

## To Roll Out Sheets:

1. Follow steps 1 through 5 for rolling strands of pasta at left.

2. Roll out the dough on the next to last setting to form a sheet the same width as the pasta maker, 24 inches long, and 1/8 inch thick. Roll out the second piece of dough in the same manner.

## To Make Ravioli or Casonsei:

1. Brush one long half of a pasta sheet with an egg. Arrange the filling in small mounds as indicated in the recipe. Gently fold the other half of the pasta dough over the top of the filling. Press the pasta dough down around each mound of filling, using your fingers or the edge of a small glass.

2. For square ravioli, use a pastry cutter or knife to cut at an even distance between the mounds. For casonsei, arrange one side of the round cookie cutter near the mound, with the other side hanging over the fold of the pasta dough to create a half circle.

## To Make Cannelloni:

After the pasta is cooked, arrange the pasta sheets on top of each other, 6 at a time, leaving a 1-inch border along the top of each sheet. Pipe out the filling onto each border and roll the pasta around the filling, beginning with the edge closest to the filling.

## To Make Cappellacci:

Cut into squares, as indicated in the recipe. Fold each square in half, corner to corner, to form a triangle. Gently place a finger on each edge to push out the air and seal the edges. (This also helps to prevent the stuffing from spilling out the sides.) Fold the uncut edge over and pull the corners around to the center to form the "hat" shape.

# BASIC GNOCCHI

This is the most common type of gnocchi. It is important to use baking potatoes for the dough because they contain less moisture than other types of potatoes. As a result, you will not need to add as much flour and will end up with a stronger potato flavor. It may take a little practice to get the knack of rolling out the dough, but your efforts will be rewarded with light, flavorful dumplings.

3 medium baking potatoes (about 9 ounces each)

1 large egg

½ teaspoon sea salt

½ teaspoon freshly ground white pepper

Pinch of freshly grated nutmeg

½ cup all-purpose flour

Preheat the oven to 450°F.

Wrap the potatoes in a double layer of aluminum foil and place in an ovenproof skillet. Bake until tender, 45 to 50 minutes. Let cool.

Peel the potatoes and press through a potato ricer onto a flat work surface. Beat the egg with a fork in a small bowl. Add the salt, pepper, and nutmeg to the egg. Pour over the potato. Sprinkle the flour over the potato and egg. Mix together, using your hands, scraping with a spatula to loosen any dough that sticks to the surface as you mix and adding flour as needed, until the dough no longer sticks to your hands. Be careful not to add too much flour.

Gently knead the pasta: push the dough away with the heels of your hands, fold it in half, give it a quarter turn, and push it away again to force out any air. Knead until the dough is completely smooth. Wash your hands with hot water to eliminate any residual flour. Roll the dough into a cylinder and cut and shape it as directed in the step-by-step guide at right.

## STEP-BY-STEP GUIDE FOR SHAPING DUMPLINGS

On a flat, flour-dusted work surface, roll the dough into a cylinder 3½ inches in diameter and 5 inches long. Cut into five 1-inch-thick slices.

Working with one at a time, set a slice on its edge and press it down to flatten it. Sprinkle with flour. Roll the dough with the palms of your hands in a forward motion—similar to moving a rolling pin—until you have formed a cylinder 13 to 15 inches long and ¾ inch in diameter.

## TO MAKE GNOCCHI, GNOCCHETTI, AND MALLOREDDUS:

Cut each cylinder into the length and shape indicated in the recipe. If instructed, press each piece against the tines on the back of a fork while gently rolling it down. Transfer to a flour-dusted plate with a spatula.

## TO MAKE SPÄTZLE:

Cut each cylinder into ¼-inch-thick slices. Because the spätzle is soft, it will flatten. As it does, turn it on its side, and then continue slicing. Using the blade of the knife, make an impression lengthwise on the edge of each slice, then, pressing down on the tip of the knife blade, push the knife backwards about 1 inch so that the spätzle rolls around the knife blade and forms a long, folded shape.

# Tomato Sauce
*Salsa di Pomodoro*

If there were a national sauce of Italy this would be it. Simple and quick to prepare, it is delicious on its own or as the base of a more complex sauce. If you have the time and the inclination, make a few batches and can them.

2 pounds ripe tomatoes, or one 28-ounce can whole peeled tomatoes with their juice

3 tablespoons olive oil

⅓ medium onion, diced

2 garlic cloves, smashed

½ dried peperoncino, broken into small pieces

6 fresh medium basil leaves, torn into small pieces

2 tablespoons chopped fresh oregano

¼ teaspoon sea salt

¼ teaspoon freshly ground pepper

If you are using fresh tomatoes: Bring 4 quarts of water to a boil in a large stockpot. Cut a small X in the bottom of each tomato. Drop the tomatoes into the boiling water and remove after 15 to 20 seconds. Let cool slightly, peel, and cut out the core. Cut each tomato in half, and using your thumb, scoop out the seeds. Cut into quarters. Set aside.

If you are using canned tomatoes: Pour the tomatoes with their juice into a large bowl and break the tomatoes into smaller pieces with your hands. Set aside.

Heat the olive oil in a medium saucepan over medium-high heat. Add the onion, garlic, and peperoncino. Cook until the onion is tender, 3 to 5 minutes. Add the tomatoes, basil, oregano, salt, and pepper. Bring to a boil, reduce the heat to a simmer, and cook, uncovered, 30 minutes. Remove from the heat and transfer to a food mill. Purée over a bowl. Use immediately or store, refrigerated, in an airtight container.

Makes approximately 2 cups

LASAGNE

SPAGHETTI

Cooking perfect pasta is an easy task if you follow a few simple guidelines that will ensure great results every time.

Never crowd the pot. Use a large pot and plenty of water to cook pasta, whether it's fresh or dry. Always begin with a large stockpot filled with 5 quarts of water and 5 teaspoons of sea salt per pound of pasta.

Never cut or break pasta. Breaking the pasta provides more surfaces that will absorb water. (Italians also don't cut cooked pasta, either, as it becomes more difficult to pick up in small pieces.)

Once the pasta is added to the pot, return the water to a boil as quickly as possible to prevent the pasta from becoming gummy. You can cover the pot until the water begins to boil, but the lid should be removed while the pasta is cooking.

Don't add oil to the water when cooking any dry pasta or most fresh ones. It defeats the purpose of the pasta—to serve as a surface to which the sauce will stick. The exception to this rule is large sheets of fresh pasta; when cooking these, it is acceptable to add a teaspoon or two of olive oil to prevent the sheets from sticking together.

Cook pasta until it is al dente; never overcook it. Pasta should retain a slight toughness in the center when it is ready to be consumed. It should never be mushy. Always taste the pasta a few minutes before the end of the cooking time printed on the package so as not to overcook it. For fresh pasta, the longer it dries, the longer it will take to cook, but again, take great care not to overcook it. Most types of fresh pasta will cook in 30 seconds to 3 minutes.

Never wash or rinse pasta. The starch that remains on the pasta acts as a thickening agent for a sauce and helps the sauce attach to the pasta.

Always reserve a small portion of the water in which the pasta was cooked. If a sauce has become too thick, a spoonful of the cooking water will thin it out.

Pasta sauce can often sit for a few minutes once it is finished, but pasta must be added to the sauce and served immediately after it is cooked. And then, of course, you must eat it right away!

In my parents' home, as in most Italian homes, meals were a sacred event. There was a certain protocol that was always observed. It began when either lunch or dinner was ready. You could set the clock by when the meal was placed on the table. And we would only begin when everyone was present.

Every meal was served at a table covered with linens, and placed in the center of the table were three carafes. One was filled with water, another with white wine, and a third with red wine. In Italy, wine is considered an essential part of a meal, and you need to have it on the table, whether you drink it or not. There were never fewer than three courses—for lunch or dinner—and pasta was almost always one of them. This is the Italian way.

Pasta is always served before the main part of the meal, as a separate course. In keeping with the traditions of Italy, the recipes in this book are designed as a first course; however, they may just as easily be served in larger portions for a main course.

In southern Italy, pasta is usually served family-style in a large bowl. In the north it is typically served on individual plates. However served, there should be only enough sauce to coat the pasta, and when the last bite of pasta is gone, the sauce should be, too.

Freshly grated cheese, black pepper, and extra-virgin olive oil are set on the table, to be added by each person according to taste. This is a matter of personal preference and no absolute rules apply. However, shellfish is rarely combined with cheese, because its subtle flavors are easily overwhelmed. In my opinion, cheese is fine on all other pasta, unless it will overpower the flavors of the other ingredients.

The most important advice I can give you about pasta is to make it a part of your life and relish it at every meal. I hope that this book will help you learn to love pasta as much as I do. So, andiamo a cucinare— "now let's cook!"

AT THE TOP OF THE BOOT

Majestic mountains, severe plains, and seaside borders—these landscapes characterize the regions at the top of boot-shaped Italy, including Liguria, Piemonte, Val d'Aosta, Lombardia, Trentino-Alto Adige, Friuli-Venezia Giulia, and Veneto. The relatively cooler climate and harsh terrain of these regions have given rise to dishes marked by concentrated flavors. Their common proximity to neighboring European countries is easily detected in their styles of cooking—many of the area's dishes can be directly linked to Germany, France, or Austria.

There is a lingering perception that Italy's northern regions are more prosperous than those in the south. This may have been true at one time. Today, the ingredients that flavor each region's signature pasta dishes are a better way to distinguish the top of the boot from the heel.

Much meat and dairy is consumed in the north because of their availability, the climate, and northern European influences. Butter, cream, and the creamy cheeses of Italy—blue-veined gorgonzola, nutty taleggio, and milky fontina—are signature ingredients of the region's traditional pasta dishes.

Many of the foods that appear in the region's most legendary fare grow low to the ground or below it and are harvested in autumn, including potatoes and the more than 250 varieties of mushrooms that populate the forests. The highly prized white truffle is the area's most exclusive and guarded culinary commodity.

The bounty of the Mediterranean and Adriatic Seas provide a profusion of seafood, from mussels to clams, prawns to calamari. Italy's northern regions showcase these treasures baked in tomato sauces, pan-roasted in buttery mixtures, and smoked for unrivaled complexity.

I have a profound appreciation for the recipes in this chapter because so many of them are nostalgic reminders of my childhood. I think you will love them because of their delicious flavors.

## LIGURIA

*Trenette con Pesto alla Genovese* 34
PASTA RIBBONS WITH PESTO,
GREEN BEANS, AND POTATOES

*Tortiglioni al Sugo di Carne* 36
RIDGED TUBES WITH A MEAT AND
PORCINI SAUCE BAKED IN A CLAY POT

*Pansoti au Preboggion* 37
PASTA STUFFED WITH A
WILD-GREENS FILLING AND TOPPED
WITH A BUTTERMILK SAUCE

## PIEMONTE E VAL D'AOSTA

*Cannelloni alla Montanara* 39
STUFFED PASTA TUBES
BAKED IN BÉCHAMEL SAUCE
WITH MUSHROOMS, TOMATOES,
AND TRUFFLES

*Tagliolini al Tartufo* 41
FRESH PASTA RIBBONS IN A
BUTTER SAUCE TOPPED WITH
SHAVED WHITE TRUFFLES

*Gnocchi Ripieni* 43
POTATO DUMPLINGS FILLED WITH
A SAUSAGE STUFFING AND
TOPPED WITH TOMATO SAUCE

*Taglierini Gratinati* 44
FRESH PASTA RIBBONS BAKED
IN A CREAM SAUCE WITH
SAUTÉED HAM AND GREEN PEAS

*Ravioli al Vino Rosso* 46
MEAT AND SPINACH–STUFFED
PASTA WITH A RED WINE SAUCE

## LOMBARDIA

### Gemelli ai Quattro Formaggi  47
TWISTED "TWIN STRANDS"
OF PASTA WITH A
FOUR-CHEESE SAUCE

### Pizzoccheri della Valtellina  48
SAVOY CABBAGE, POTATOES,
FONTINA CHEESE, AND
BUCKWHEAT NOODLES
BAKED IN A CASSEROLE

### Gnocchi Gratinati al Gorgonzola  50
POTATO DUMPLINGS BAKED
IN A GORGONZOLA SAUCE

### Casonsei alla Bergamasca  51
PASTA STUFFED WITH AN
ANISE-FLAVORED FILLING

### Penne Vodka  53
RIBBED PASTA TUBES IN A
CREAMY TOMATO-VODKA SAUCE

## TRENTINO-ALTO ADIGE

### Farfalle al Salmone  54
BOW-TIE PASTA IN A
SMOKED SALMON, CAPER,
AND BRANDY CREAM SAUCE

### Spätzle Crema e Speck  56
SPINACH DUMPLINGS WITH
A HAM AND CREAM SAUCE

### Canederli Tirolesi  59
A TRIO OF SPINACH,
MUSHROOM, AND RICOTTA-
PANCETTA DUMPLINGS
SERVED IN CHICKEN STOCK

## FRIULI-VENEZIA GIULIA

### Offelle alla Triestina  62
POTATO RAVIOLI FILLED
WITH SPINACH AND SAUSAGE
AND TOPPED WITH
BROWN BUTTER AND SAGE

### Vermicelli alla Busara  65
SAUTÉED PRAWNS WITH
CAPERS, CREAM, AND
TOMATO SAUCE OVER
THIN PASTA STRANDS

## VENETO

### Casonsei Ampezzani  66
BEET-FLAVORED PASTA
STUFFED WITH A
RICOTTA-BEET FILLING
TOPPED WITH BROWN BUTTER
AND POPPY SEEDS

### Spaghettini in Salsa alla Trevisana  68
THIN PASTA STRANDS IN A
TOMATO-ANCHOVY SAUCE

### Bigoli in Casso Pipa  69
SEAFOOD BAKED IN
A TOMATO SAUCE WITH
ROUND PASTA STRANDS

### Pasticcio di Pesce  71
FRESH PASTA BAKED IN A
CREAMY SEAFOOD SAUCE

### Gnocchi alle Melanzane  73
EGGPLANT-POTATO
DUMPLINGS TOPPED WITH A
TOMATO-BASIL SAUCE

### Boccon del Prete  74
RICOTTA-SPINACH DUMPLINGS
BAKED IN A CREAMY
PORCINI MUSHROOM SAUCE

### Rigatoni alla Crudaiola  76
FAT PASTA TUBES IN A FRESH
TOMATO AND OLIVE SAUCE

### Gnocchetti con Calamari e Radicchio  77
POTATO DUMPLINGS WITH
CALAMARI AND RADICCHIO

# PASTA RIBBONS WITH PESTO, GREEN BEANS, AND POTATOES
## Trenette con Pesto alla Genovese

SERVES 6

This classic Ligurian dish features pesto, a condiment dating back to Roman times and thought to have originated in Genoa. This particular recipe is from a town called Camogli, where pesto includes a cheese called cagliata, a fresh cow's milk cheese with a spreadable consistency. I've substituted crème fraîche because it tastes similar to cagliata, which is difficult to find in the United States.

50 fresh medium basil leaves, washed and dried thoroughly

3 garlic cloves

¾ cup freshly grated Parmigiano-Reggiano

⅓ cup freshly grated Pecorino Romano

2 tablespoons pine nuts, lightly toasted

½ cup extra-virgin olive oil

5 ½ teaspoons sea salt

¼ teaspoon freshly ground pepper

1 tablespoon crème fraîche

½ pound Yukon gold potatoes, peeled, quartered, and cut into ½-inch-thick slices

¼ pound green beans, cut into 1-inch lengths

1 pound dry trenette

Place the basil in the bowl of a food processor and chop fine. Add the garlic and continue chopping. Add the parmigiano, pecorino, and pine nuts and process until the nuts are chopped fine. Gradually add the olive oil while the motor is running. Add ½ teaspoon of the salt and the pepper and pulse to combine. Add the crème fraîche and pulse to combine. Do not over-process; it should all be blended within 3 to 5 minutes.

Bring 5 quarts of water and the remaining 5 teaspoons of salt to a boil. Add the potatoes and return to a boil. Add the beans and pasta and cook until the pasta is al dente.

Heat the pesto in a large sauté pan with 1 to 2 tablespoons of the cooking water from the pasta. Do not boil. Transfer the pasta, beans, and potatoes to a colander to drain, reserving 1 cup of the water. Add the pasta to the pan with the pesto and toss to coat evenly. Add the reserved water, if needed. Toss to mix well. Twist the noodles into a mound on each individual plate.

## Tortiglioni al Sugo di Carne

◎

1 ounce dried porcini
mushrooms

1 cup hot water

Flour for dredging

One 3-pound boneless
beef chuck roast, cut
into 4 pieces

1/4 cup plus 4 tablespoons
olive oil

5 teaspoons sea salt,
plus extra for seasoning

1/4 teaspoon freshly
ground pepper, plus
extra for seasoning

1 tablespoon
unsalted butter

1 yellow onion, diced

4 garlic cloves, smashed

1/3 cup pine nuts

1 tablespoon chopped
fresh marjoram

1/2 cup dry red wine

1 pound dry tortiglioni

1/3 cup freshly grated
Parmigiano-Reggiano

*Fresh porcini mushrooms can be difficult to find in the United States, and those that are available often have a weak taste. This wintry dish relies on the robust flavor of the mushrooms, so dried porcini are ideal because of their concentrated flavor. The liquid from rehydrating them is added for greater complexity. This dish is best made with a clay pot. If you don't have one, use a Dutch oven.*

Preheat the oven to 400°F.

Place the porcini in a small bowl and cover with the hot water. Let sit 30 minutes. Remove the porcini from the water with your hands and transfer to a colander to drain. Strain the soaking liquid to eliminate any sand and reserve. Squeeze the porcini to eliminate any excess liquid. Chop and set aside.

Put the clay pot without the lid in the oven to heat it.

Place the flour in a shallow bowl. Add the beef and turn to coat evenly. Heat 1/4 cup of the olive oil in a large sauté pan. Shake any excess flour off of the beef and add the beef to the pan. Cook until browned on both sides, about 3 minutes per side. Sprinkle the beef with a generous amount of salt and pepper. Transfer to a plate and discard the oil.

Remove the clay pot from the oven and add 2 tablespoons of olive oil, the butter, onion, and garlic. Bake until the onion is browned, 3 to 5 minutes. Add the porcini, pine nuts, and half of the marjoram. Bake until the nuts are browned, about 5 minutes. Add the meat and bake 5 minutes more. Add the wine, cover, and bake until reduced by half, about 15 minutes. Add the reserved porcini liquid, a pinch of salt, and the 1/4 teaspoon of pepper. Cover and cook until the liquid is reduced by half again, 5 to 10 minutes. Transfer the solid ingredients to a cutting board and chop into a coarse mixture. Put them in a large sauté pan along with the reduced liquid in the clay pot and heat over medium heat.

Bring 5 quarts of water and the 5 teaspoons of sea salt to a boil in a large stockpot over high heat. Add the pasta and cook until al dente. Transfer to a colander to drain. Add to the pan with the meat sauce and toss to coat evenly. Add the parmigiano and the remaining 2 tablespoons olive oil. Sprinkle with the remaining marjoram. Toss to mix well.

# Pasta Stuffed with a Wild-Greens Filling and Topped with a Buttermilk Sauce

*Pansoti au Preboggion*

SERVES 6

This ravioli is named for its plump center. The Italian word pansa, means "belly." Preboggion refers to the European herb borage, an ingredient originally used in the filling. Pansoti au Preboggion were traditionally prepared with wild greens foraged from the surrounding countryside. Since few of us gather wild foods these days, a mixture of earthy greens is a suitable substitution.

To make the pasta: Prepare the pasta dough as directed on page 21. Let sit 30 minutes.

Bring 5 quarts of water and the 5 teaspoons of salt to a boil in a large stockpot over high heat.

Add the dandelion greens, chard, kale, and greens; cook until wilted, about 5 minutes. Transfer to a colander to drain. Squeeze to eliminate any excess liquid.

Heat the butter and oil in a large sauté pan over medium-high heat until the butter melts, about 2 minutes. Add the onion and garlic and cook until tender, about 5 minutes. Add the greens mixture and cook 10 to 15 minutes. Let cool. Squeeze to eliminate any excess liquid.

Transfer the greens mixture to the bowl of a food processor. Add the parmigiano and 1 egg. Process until a fine mixture is achieved. Add the ricotta and pulse to combine. Season with a pinch of salt and pepper. Set aside.

Roll out the pasta as described in steps 1 and 2 under "To roll out sheets" on page 22. Beat the remaining egg in a small bowl with a fork. Brush each sheet of dough with the egg. Cut each one into 2 1/2-inch squares, using a fluted pastry cutter. Arrange the filling in small mounds (about 1 tablespoon each) in the center of each square. One at a time, fold a square in half, corner to corner, to form a triangle. Gently place one finger on each edge to push out the air and seal the edges. (This also helps to prevent the stuffing from spilling out the sides.) Transfer the pansoti to a flour-dusted platter and sprinkle with a light coating of flour.

To make the sauce: Place the bread in a medium bowl. Pour the water over the bread and let sit until absorbed, about 15 minutes. Squeeze out any excess liquid. Put the walnuts in the bowl of a food processor and chop until fine. Transfer a small amount to a bowl and reserve. Add the garlic to the bowl of the food processor and finely chop. Add the bread, buttermilk, and parmigiano. Process until a smooth paste forms. With the motor running, gradually add the olive oil. Transfer the sauce to a large sauté pan and heat over medium heat. Season with salt and pepper.

Bring 5 quarts of water and the 5 teaspoons of salt to a boil in a large stockpot over high heat.

Add the pasta and cook until the pansoti rise to the top, 3 to 5 minutes. Transfer to a colander to drain, reserving some of the water for the sauce. If the sauce appears to be too thick, add enough cooking water to achieve a liquid consistency. Add the pasta and toss to combine. Top with the reserved chopped walnuts and the parsley.

Note: Black kale, *cavalo nero*, is actually black cabbage, and is similar to kale. Look for it in the produce department of specialty markets. If you aren't able to locate it, kale can be used.

## For the pasta:

1 recipe Basic Pasta (page 21)

5 teaspoons sea salt, plus extra for seasoning

1 cup chopped dandelion greens

1 cup chopped Swiss chard

1 cup chopped black kale (see Note)

1 cup chopped greens (such as spinach, collard greens, or mustard greens)

3 tablespoons unsalted butter

2 tablespoons olive oil

1/2 small white onion, diced

6 garlic cloves, chopped

1 cup freshly grated Parmigiano-Reggiano

2 large eggs

1 cup ricotta

Freshly ground pepper

## For the sauce:

3 cups stale bread cubes (about 1/2 pound)

1 cup water

1/2 cup walnuts

3 garlic cloves

1 cup buttermilk

1/2 cup freshly grated Parmigiano-Reggiano

1/3 cup extra-virgin olive oil

5 teaspoons sea salt

2 tablespoons chopped fresh Italian parsley

## STUFFED PASTA TUBES BAKED IN BÉCHAMEL SAUCE WITH MUSHROOMS, TOMATOES, AND TRUFFLES
### *Cannelloni alla Montanara*

◉

SERVES 6

*Y*ou can divide this dish down the center and credit both the Piemonte region and the bordering country of France for its composition. The mushrooms and truffles are quintessential Piemonte ingredients, and the veal and béchamel reflect the influence of French cuisine. As you may know, Piemonte is world famous for its white truffles, but black truffles, which flavor this dish, are also grown in the region.

Prepare the pasta dough as directed on page 21. Let sit 30 minutes.

To make the béchamel sauce: Slowly bring the milk to a low boil in a medium saucepan over medium-low heat. Melt the butter in a large saucepan over medium heat. Add the flour to the butter and cook, stirring, until the flour is well incorporated, about 2 minutes. Whisk in the milk, nutmeg, salt, and pepper. Cook until the mixture becomes thick, about 10 minutes, stirring frequently. Remove from the heat. Drizzle a small amount of olive oil over the top of the sauce to prevent a skin from forming.

To make the filling: Heat 1/4 cup of the olive oil in a large sauté pan over medium-high heat. Add the veal, pancetta, rosemary, sage, and garlic. Cook until the veal is browned, about 10 minutes. Add the wine and cook until the liquid is nearly evaporated, about 5 minutes. Drain the excess fat from the pan by tilting the pan and spooning out the oil that has collected on the side. Transfer the veal mixture to the bowl of a food processor. Pulse to chop into a coarse mixture. Wipe out the sauté pan and return it to the stove.

Heat the remaining 1/4 cup of olive oil in the sauté pan over medium-high heat. Add the

carrot, onion, and celery. Cook until tender, about 10 minutes. Transfer to a bowl. Add the meat mixture, 1/2 cup of the béchamel, the salt, and white pepper. Mix well. Taste and adjust the seasoning with additional salt and pepper. Transfer the filling to a pastry bag with a 1-inch opening. Set aside.

Preheat the oven to 350°F.

Roll out the pasta as described in steps 1 and 2 under "To roll out sheets" on page 22. Cut each 24-inch pasta sheet into six 4-inch squares. Bring 5 quarts of water and the 5 teaspoons of salt to a boil in a large stockpot over high heat. Add the pasta, 6 squares at time, and cook 2 to 3 minutes. Transfer to a colander to drain.

Spread a small amount of olive oil on a flat work surface. Arrange a pasta sheet on the surface. Sprinkle lightly with 2 teaspoons of the parmigiano and then stack a second sheet over it so that there is a 1-inch border at the top.

(continued on next page)

---

1 recipe Basic Pasta
(page 21)

*For the béchamel sauce:*

4 cups milk

1/2 cup (1 stick)
unsalted butter

1/2 cup all-purpose flour

1/2 teaspoon freshly
grated nutmeg

1/2 teaspoon sea salt

1/2 teaspoon freshly
ground white pepper

Olive oil for drizzling

*For the filling:*

1/2 cup olive oil

3/4 pound veal stew meat

1/3 pound pancetta,
chopped

1 tablespoon chopped
fresh rosemary

8 fresh sage leaves

2 garlic cloves, smashed

1/2 cup dry red wine

1 medium carrot,
finely diced

1/2 small onion,
finely diced

1/2 celery stalk,
finely diced

1 teaspoon sea salt

1/2 teaspoon freshly ground
white pepper

*(ingredients continued
on next page)*

*5 teaspoons sea salt*

*¾ cup freshly grated
Parmigiano-Reggiano*

*For the topping:*

*½ cup olive oil*

*8 medium button
mushrooms, sliced*

*1 garlic clove, smashed*

*2 tablespoons chopped
fresh Italian parsley*

*2 ripe medium tomatoes,
peeled, seeded, and
finely diced*

*4 fresh large basil leaves,
torn into small pieces*

*¼ teaspoon sea salt*

*1 black truffle or
1 teaspoon black truffle oil*

Continue in this fashion until all 6 sheets are stacked on the work surface, and the top of each is 1 inch from that of the preceding layer (like flattened stairs). Pipe out equal amounts of the filling on the 1-inch border of each pasta sheet. Beginning with the pasta sheet closest to you, roll the pasta around the filling: start with the edge closest to the filling and roll toward the opposite edge. Press firmly to create a smooth cylinder. Repeat with the remaining pasta sheets. Cut the edges off each roll with a sharp knife. Drizzle a small amount of olive oil in the bottom of a 10-by-14-inch baking dish. Spread a spoonful of the béchamel over the olive oil and place a layer of the filled cannelloni in the baking dish. They should fit snugly. Spread the remaining béchamel over the cannelloni. Sprinkle with the remaining parmigiano. Bake until crispy, 15 to 20 minutes.

While the cannelloni are baking, make the topping: Heat ¼ cup of the olive oil in a large sauté pan over high heat. Add the mushrooms and garlic. Cook until the mushrooms are crispy, about 10 minutes. Remove the garlic and add 1 tablespoon of the parsley. Mix well. Spread over the cannelloni, creating a stripe that covers a third of the baking dish. Return the sauté pan to the stove and add the remaining ¼ cup of olive oil. Add the tomatoes, basil, and salt. Cook until tender, about 3 minutes. Spread alongside the mushrooms, to make another stripe over the cannelloni. Spread the sliced truffle next to the tomato or drizzle the truffle oil over the whole casserole. Sprinkle with the remaining 1 tablespoon of parsley.

### Leftovers

When you make this dish you will inevitably have extra pasta and filling. Both of these can be enjoyed at another meal. Cook the few strips of remaining pasta as directed in the recipe and set in a small gratin dish. Mix in the filling. Top with a bit of melted butter or béchamel, parmigiano, salt, and pepper and place under the broiler. It makes a wonderful lunch or dinner for one. You can do the same with your leftovers from any stuffed pasta dish.

# FRESH PASTA RIBBONS IN A BUTTER SAUCE
## TOPPED WITH SHAVED WHITE TRUFFLES
*Tagliolini al Tartufo*

SERVES 4

This recipe showcases the intense, earthy taste of white truffles. Indigenous to Piemonte, they have a short season. This dish should only be made when fresh white truffles are available. It is a crime to eat it any other way.

Prepare the pasta as directed on page 21. Let rest 30 minutes.

Roll out the pasta dough into two 48-inch sheets as described in steps 1 to 6 under "To roll out strands and ribbons" on page 22. Cut each 48-inch sheet crosswise into four 12-inch lengths. Using the pasta maker attachment, cut each sheet into flat ribbons 1/16 inch wide. Transfer to a flour-dusted platter and sprinkle with additional flour. Let dry at least 2 hours, moving the pasta occasionally to prevent sticking.

Bring the wine to a boil in a large sauté pan. Cook until nearly evaporated. Add the water and 1/2 teaspoon of the salt and return to a boil. Cook until reduced to a third, about 5 minutes. Whisk in the butter and cook until melted, but don't boil. Add the pepper. Season with salt.

Bring 5 quarts of water and the remaining 5 teaspoons of salt to a boil in a large stockpot over high heat. Add the pasta and cook until al dente, 30 seconds to 3 minutes, depending on how dry the pasta is. Taste to prevent overcooking. Transfer to a colander to drain.

Add 1 cup of the parmigiano to the wine sauce. Add the pasta and toss to mix well. Add the remaining 1/2 cup of parmigiano and the truffle oil and stir gently. Using a large fork and spoon, pick up a portion of the pasta with the fork and twirl it against the spoon to form a mound, then arrange on an individual plate. Mound the remaining servings on plates and shave an equal amount of the truffle over each one.

## Truffle Care

White truffles are a delicate food that should be treated with great care. Wrap fresh truffles in a paper towel and store in a cool, dry place, or in the refrigerator. You can also cover them with rice and store in an airtight container in the refrigerator. To prepare truffles for use, brush away any dirt then clean with a damp paper towel. To slice, use a truffle shaver for paper-thin slices. A vegetable peeler is an acceptable but less efficient tool. Never cook a white truffle; the heat will destroy its flavor.

1 recipe Basic Pasta
(page 21)

1/2 cup dry white wine

1 cup water

5 1/2 teaspoons sea salt,
plus extra for seasoning

3/4 cup (1 1/2 sticks)
unsalted butter, cut
into pieces

1/2 teaspoon freshly ground
white pepper

1 1/2 cups freshly grated
Parmigiano-Reggiano

1 teaspoon white truffle oil

1 medium white truffle

# Potato Dumplings Filled with a Sausage Stuffing and Topped with Tomato Sauce
## Gnocchi Ripieni

SERVES 6

Gnocchi are among the oldest foods in Italy; they reportedly first appeared in the kitchens of ancient Rome. Today they are prepared all over the country, but this stuffed version is usually made only in Piemonte.

Preheat the oven to 450°F.

Wrap the potatoes in a double layer of aluminum foil and place in an ovenproof skillet. Bake until tender, about 1 hour and 30 minutes. Let cool.

While the potatoes are cooking, heat 2 tablespoons of the olive oil in a large sauté pan over medium-high heat. Add the sausage and cook until browned, about 5 minutes. Add the shallot and cook until soft, about 5 minutes. Add 1/4 teaspoon of the salt and the pepper. Add the wine and cook until completely evaporated, 3 to 5 minutes. Transfer the mixture to a colander to drain and put in the bowl of a food processor. Add the cream and egg yolk. Process until a fine mixture is achieved. Transfer to a pastry bag with a 1-inch tip.

Peel the potatoes and press through a potato ricer onto a flat work surface. Sprinkle 1/4 cup of the flour, 1 tablespoon of the thyme, the rosemary, and sage over the potato. Beat the egg with a fork in a small bowl. Pour over the potato. Mix together, using your hands, scraping with a spatula to loosen any dough that sticks to the surface as you mix and adding flour as needed, until the dough no longer sticks to your hands. Gently knead the pasta until it is smooth. Wash your hands with hot water to eliminate any residual flour.

Divide the dough in half and roll each portion into a long cylinder, 2 inches in diameter. Dust your hands with flour to prevent sticking and, using the edge of one hand, make an indentation down the center of one of the cylinders. Shape the sides to form a canoe-shaped strip of pasta with 1-inch-high sides and a 1-inch-wide base. Pipe half the filling down the center of the pasta in a continuous motion to fill in the hollow. Gather the edges together and press to seal. Roll into a cylinder 1/2 to 3/4 inch in diameter. Dust with flour. Cut into 1/2-inch-thick slices, using a very sharp knife. Fill and roll the second cylinder in the same fashion.

Heat the remaining 1/4 cup of olive oil in a large sauté pan over medium-high heat. Add the diced tomatoes and remaining 2 tablespoons of thyme. Add the tomato sauce and bring to a boil. Reduce the heat to low and keep warm while the pasta is cooking.

Bring 5 quarts of water and the remaining 5 teaspoons of salt to a boil in a large stockpot over high heat. Add the gnocchi and cook until they rise to the top, 5 to 10 minutes. Transfer to a colander to drain. Add to the pan with the tomato sauce and toss to mix well. Sprinkle with the parmigiano.

---

3 medium baking potatoes (about 3/4 pound each)

1/4 cup plus 2 tablespoons olive oil

3/4 pound mild Italian sausage, crumbled

1 large shallot, minced

5 1/4 teaspoons sea salt

1/4 teaspoon freshly ground pepper

1/2 cup dry red wine

1 tablespoon heavy whipping cream

1 egg yolk

1/4 to 1/2 cup all-purpose flour

3 tablespoons minced fresh thyme

1 tablespoon minced fresh rosemary

1 tablespoon minced fresh sage

1 large egg

1 medium tomato, peeled, seeded, and cut into 1/4-inch dice

2 cups Salsa di Pomodoro (page 24)

1/2 cup freshly grated Parmigiano-Reggiano

# FRESH PASTA RIBBONS BAKED IN A CREAM SAUCE
## WITH SAUTÉED HAM AND GREEN PEAS
*Taglierini Gratinati*

◎

SERVES 6

The simplicity of this pasta belies the satisfaction each bite brings. The key to this dish is to cook the ham until it is crispy, to achieve the right textural impact on the palate.

1 recipe Basic Pasta
(page 21)

2 tablespoons olive oil

2 tablespoons
unsalted butter

6 ounces ham, julienned

¼ medium onion, chopped

1 cup shelled fresh peas

1 tablespoon chopped
fresh Italian parsley

1 cup dry white wine

1 cup heavy
whipping cream

5 teaspoons sea salt,
plus extra for seasoning

Freshly ground pepper

½ cup freshly grated
Parmigiano-Reggiano

Prepare the pasta as directed on page 21. Let sit 30 minutes.

Roll out the pasta dough into two 48-inch sheets as described in steps 1 to 6 under "To roll out strands and ribbons" on page 22. Cut each 48-inch sheet crosswise into four 12-inch lengths. Using the pasta maker attachment, cut each sheet into flat ribbons ⅛ inch wide. Lay on a flat work surface and dust with flour. Dry at least 2 hours.

Preheat the broiler.

Heat the olive oil and butter in a large sauté pan over medium-high heat. Add the ham and cook until crispy, 3 to 5 minutes. Add the onion and cook 2 minutes. Add the peas and parsley; cook until the peas are barely tender, about 2 minutes. Add the wine. Cook until reduced by a third, 3 to 5 minutes. Add the cream. Add a pinch of salt and pepper; bring to a boil and cook until reduced by half, 3 to 5 minutes.

Bring 5 quarts of water and the 5 teaspoons of salt to a boil over high heat. Add the pasta and cook until al dente, 30 seconds to 1 minute, depending on how dry the pasta is. Taste to prevent overcooking. Transfer to a colander to drain. Add to the pan with the ham and pea sauce and toss to coat evenly. Transfer to a shallow baking dish, cover with the parmigiano, and set under the broiler until browned, about 3 minutes.

*Ravioli al Vino Rosso*

---

1 recipe Basic Pasta
(page 21)

¼ cup olive oil

1 garlic clove, smashed

½ small carrot, diced

½ small celery
stalk, diced

¼ medium onion, diced

½ pound beef stew meat

2 tablespoons chopped
fresh rosemary

8 fresh sage leaves

2 bay leaves

2 ¾ cups high-quality,
dry red wine

1 cup water

6 ounces baby
spinach leaves

2 ounces prosciutto,
chopped

5 ½ teaspoons sea salt

¼ teaspoon freshly
ground pepper

1 egg, beaten

1 teaspoon whole
black peppercorns

2 tablespoons
unsalted butter

2 tablespoons chopped
fresh Italian parsley

Freshly grated
Parmigiano-Reggiano

**B**orn in the cold climate of Piemonte, this dish warms the body and soul. The wine is the star of the sauce, so use a good red, or the taste will be disappointing. Consider a high-quality, young Barbera from Italy or a Merlot or Cabernet Sauvignon from California for the best sauce.

Prepare the pasta as directed on page 21. Let sit 30 minutes.

Heat the olive oil in a large sauté pan over medium-high heat. Add the garlic and cook 1 minute. Add the carrot, celery, and onion and cook 2 minutes. Add the beef, rosemary, sage, and 1 bay leaf. Cook until the beef is browned on all sides, 15 to 20 minutes. Add ¾ cup of the red wine. Cook until completely evaporated, about 5 minutes. Add the water and cook until nearly evaporated, about 5 minutes. Add the spinach and cook until tender, about 5 minutes more. Remove the bay leaf. Transfer the beef mixture to the bowl of a food processor and add the prosciutto. Chop until a fine mixture is achieved. Add ¼ teaspoon of the salt and the pepper. Transfer to a pastry bag with a 1-inch tip.

Roll out the pasta as described in steps 1 and 2 under "To roll out sheets" on page 22. Brush one long half of a pasta sheet with some of the beaten egg. Pipe out (or drop by the spoonful) 12 small mounds (about 2 teaspoons each) of the filling, spacing them about 2 inches apart, down the center of the egg-brushed half. Fold the other pasta half over, forming a long rectangle, and gently push the pasta down around each mound to push out any air. Cut into 2-inch squares with a fluted pastry cutter. Transfer to a platter dusted with flour. Repeat with the remaining pasta and filling.

Bring the remaining 2 cups of red wine to a boil over high heat. Whisk in the peppercorns, ¼ teaspoon of the salt, and the remaining bay leaf. Cook until reduced by half, about 5 minutes, and strain. Whisk in the butter.

Bring 5 quarts of water and the remaining 5 teaspoons of sea salt to a boil in a large stockpot over high heat. Add the ravioli and cook until tender, 2 to 3 minutes. Transfer to a colander to drain. Add to the pan with the wine sauce and stir gently to mix. Cook 1 to 2 minutes. Transfer to a serving platter. Sprinkle with the parsley. Serve with parmigiano on the side.

# TWISTED "TWIN STRANDS" OF PASTA WITH A FOUR-CHEESE SAUCE
## Gemelli ai Quattro Formaggi

SERVES 6

Lombardia is the birthplace of mascarpone and gorgonzola, the two rich cheeses that in this dish provide a creamy backdrop for the pasta and asparagus. We often feature this pasta on our menu at Il Fornaio in the wintertime; people love its warming effects.

Heat the olive oil in a large sauté pan over medium-high heat. Add the shallot and asparagus and cook 1 to 2 minutes. Add the wine and bring to a boil. Cook until evaporated, about 3 minutes. Add the cream and a pinch of salt. Bring to a boil. Reduce the heat to low. Add the fontina and gorgonzola and cook until the consistency becomes thick, about 5 minutes.

Bring 5 quarts of water and the 5 teaspoons of salt to a boil in a large stockpot over high heat. Add the pasta and cook until al dente. Transfer to a colander to drain. Add to the pan with the cheese sauce. Add the mascarpone and parmigiano; toss to mix well. Sprinkle with freshly ground pepper.

Note: To trim the asparagus most effectively, bend each stalk at the point where it breaks easily and snap off the end. Discard the woody bottom section.

1 tablespoon olive oil

1 small shallot, minced

1 bunch large asparagus (about 1 ½ pounds), trimmed and cut on the diagonal into 2-inch pieces

¾ cup dry white wine

3 cups heavy whipping cream

5 teaspoons sea salt, plus extra for seasoning

4 ounces Italian fontina, diced

2 ounces Italian gorgonzola, cut into small pieces

1 pound dry gemelli

½ cup mascarpone

1 ½ cups freshly grated Parmigiano-Reggiano

Freshly ground pepper

# SAVOY CABBAGE, POTATOES, FONTINA CHEESE, AND BUCKWHEAT NOODLES BAKED IN A CASSEROLE

*Pizzoccheri della Valtellina*

---

SERVES 6

1 cup buckwheat flour

½ cup all-purpose flour

5 ½ teaspoons sea salt, plus extra for seasoning

1 large egg at room temperature

¼ cup milk

1 medium potato (about ¾ pound), cut into ½-inch cubes

1 small savoy cabbage (about ½ pound), cored and cut into strips ½ inch wide by 2 inches long

½ cup (1 stick) unsalted butter

12 fresh sage leaves

Freshly ground pepper

8 ounces Italian fontina, cut into ½-inch cubes

½ cup freshly grated Parmigiano-Reggiano

This rustic casserole made with wide pasta noodles is reminiscent of hard times. Its composition represents the most basic farm produce of Lombardia, and it was often consumed during the world wars, when other foods were difficult to obtain.

In a large shallow bowl or on a flat work surface, mix the buckwheat and all-purpose flours with ½ teaspoon of the salt and shape into a mound. Make a well in the center. Crack the egg into the well and add the milk. Beat with a fork, gradually beating a wider path and incorporating the flour in very small amounts. Continue mixing with the fork until the pasta begins to resemble a dry, crumbly mixture. Transfer to a flat work surface dusted with flour. Begin kneading by hand, rolling the dough sideways across the surface from hand to hand, and applying strong pressure while squeezing the dough. If the pasta is sticky, dust it with flour while kneading. Continue kneading until all of the flour is incorporated, no floury white spots remain, and the pasta begins to soften, about 10 minutes. Shape into a ball, cover with plastic wrap, and let sit 30 minutes. (This allows the flour to continue to absorb moisture from the eggs.)

Roll out the pasta as described in steps 1 and 2 under "To roll out sheets" on page 22. Cut each sheet into six 4-inch squares. Stack the squares on top of one another and cut into ¾-inch-wide strips. Transfer to a flour-dusted platter and let dry at least 2 hours.

Preheat the oven to 450°F. Butter a 13-by-9-by-2-inch baking dish.

Bring 5 quarts of water and the remaining 5 teaspoons of salt to a boil in a large stockpot over high heat. Add the potato and cook until slightly tender, about 2 minutes. Add the cabbage and cook until tender, about 3 minutes. Add the pasta and cook 1 minute more. Transfer the pasta and vegetables to a colander to drain.

Melt the butter in a large sauté pan over medium-high heat. Add the sage and cook until crispy and the butter begins to brown, about 5 minutes. Remove from the heat.

Arrange half of the pasta mixture in the prepared baking dish. Sprinkle with salt and pepper. Arrange half of the fontina over the pasta mixture and top with half of the parmigiano. Spoon half of the butter with the sage leaves over the casserole. Add the remaining pasta mixture to the baking dish. Top with the remaining fontina, parmigiano, and butter. Sprinkle with salt and pepper, and bake until the cheese melts and the top becomes crispy and browned, about 10 minutes.

# POTATO DUMPLINGS BAKED IN A GORGONZOLA SAUCE
## Gnocchi Gratinati al Gorgonzola

⊙

SERVES 6

Populated by dairy cows, the landscape of Lombardia is captured in this cheesy, creamy pasta gratin. It makes a hearty main course when accompanied by a crisp green salad and good bread.

1 recipe Basic Gnocchi
(page 23)

1 cup heavy
whipping cream

2 ounces Italian
gorgonzola, crumbled

2 ounces Italian fontina or
taleggio, cut into cubes

1/2 cup freshly grated
Parmigiano-Reggiano

5 1/4 teaspoons sea salt

1/4 teaspoon freshly
ground pepper

Prepare the gnocchi dough and roll it into a 5-inch-long cylinder and then 5 longer cylinders, as directed in the Step-by-Step Guide for Shaping Dumplings on page 23. Cut into 3/4-inch pieces. Press each piece against the tines on the back of a fork while gently rolling it down. Transfer to a flour-dusted plate with a spatula.

Preheat the broiler.

Bring the cream to a slow boil in a large sauté pan over medium heat. Cook until the cream is reduced by half, about 5 minutes. Add the gorgonzola, fontina, and 1/4 cup of the parmigiano. Cook until the cheese melts and the sauce becomes thick, about 5 minutes. Add 1/4 teaspoon of the salt and the pepper.

Bring 5 quarts of water and the remaining 5 teaspoons of salt to a boil in a large stockpot over high heat. Add the gnocchi and cook until they rise to the top, about 20 seconds. Transfer to a colander to drain. Add to the cheese sauce and stir to mix well. Transfer to an 18-by-12-by-2-inch gratin or ceramic baking dish. Sprinkle with the remaining 1/4 cup of parmigiano and place under the broiler until browned, 3 to 5 minutes.

# PASTA STUFFED WITH AN ANISE-FLAVORED FILLING
## *Casonsei alla Bergamasca*

◎

SERVES 6

All over Italy the shape and filling of casonsei vary. In the Bergamo area, near Milan, this pasta is shaped like a large flower and most likely acquired its sweet flavor from the people of this region, who supposedly have a sweet tooth. I've created a luscious cream sauce to complement the filling. This pasta is equally delicious with a brown butter and sage sauce.

Prepare the pasta as directed on page 21. Let sit 30 minutes.

To make the filling: Cut the pork and beef into 1-inch cubes. Heat the olive oil in a large sauté pan over medium-high heat. Add the pork, beef, salt, and pepper. Cook until browned, about 10 minutes. Drain the excess fat from the pan by tilting the pan and spooning out the oil collected on the side. Add the onion and garlic and cook until tender, 1 to 2 minutes. Add 1/2 cup of the wine and cook until completely evaporated, about 3 minutes. Transfer to the bowl of a food processor and add the nutmeg. Chop until a fine mixture is achieved. Do not purée. Add the parmigiano and cookies and pulse to combine. Season with salt and pepper. If too dry, add the remaining 1 tablespoon of wine. Transfer the mixture to a pastry bag with a 1-inch opening.

Roll out the pasta as described in steps 1 and 2 under "To roll out sheets" on page 22. Brush one long half of a pasta sheet with some of the beaten egg. Pipe out (or drop by the spoonfuls) 9 small mounds (about 1 tablespoon each), 2 1/2 inches apart in the center of the egg-brushed side. Fold over the other pasta half and press the dough around each mound of filling. Cut out half-moon shapes using a 2 1/2-inch fluted cookie

cutter. Fold under 1/4 inch of the straight edge and press the sides together where they meet (use a little water if needed to help make stick together). If the pasta sticks to the counter, slide a flat spatula or knife under the pasta. Transfer to a flour-dusted platter. Repeat with the remaining pasta and filling.

To make the sauce: Heat the butter and sage in a large nonstick sauté pan over medium-high heat. Cook until the butter begins to brown, 3 to 5 minutes. Add the wine and cook until reduced by half, 1 to 2 minutes. Add the cream and parmigiano. Season with salt and pepper. Bring to a boil. Reduce the heat to low and keep warm while the pasta is cooking.

Bring 5 quarts of water and the 5 teaspoons of salt to a boil in a large stockpot over high heat. Add the pasta and cook until the casonsei rise to the top, about 2 to 4 minutes. Transfer to a colander to drain. Add to the pan with the cream sauce and toss to coat evenly. Transfer to a serving dish and decorate with the tomatoes and parsley.

1 recipe Basic Pasta
(page 21)

*For the filling:*

1/4 pound pork butt

1/4 pound beef stew meat

1/3 cup olive oil

1/2 teaspoon sea salt, plus extra for seasoning

1/4 teaspoon freshly ground pepper, plus extra for seasoning

1/2 small onion, chopped

2 garlic cloves, smashed

1/2 cup plus 1 tablespoon dry white wine

1/2 teaspoon freshly grated nutmeg

1/2 cup freshly grated Parmigiano-Reggiano

1/3 cup crumbled amaretti cookies (about 6 whole)

1 egg, beaten

*For the sauce:*

2 tablespoons unsalted butter

12 fresh sage leaves

1/2 cup dry white wine

2 cups heavy whipping cream

1/2 cup freshly grated Parmigiano-Reggiano

5 teaspoons sea salt, plus extra for seasoning

Freshly ground pepper

1 medium tomato, peeled, seeded, and cut into 1/4-inch dice

2 tablespoons chopped fresh Italian parley

## RIBBED PASTA TUBES IN A
## CREAMY TOMATO-VODKA SAUCE
### Penne Vodka

*Many people are surprised by the inclusion of vodka in this traditional pasta recipe. Bordering so many other European countries, Italy has long been influenced by other cultures, such as Russia and Poland, where vodka originates.*

Heat 2 tablespoons of the olive oil in a large non-stick sauté pan over medium-high heat. Add the pancetta and cook until crispy, about 5 minutes. Drain the excess fat from the pan by tilting the pan and spooning out the oil collected on the side. Add the remaining 1 tablespoon of olive oil and heat over medium-high heat. Add the shallots and cook until soft, about 3 minutes. Add the vodka. Bring to a boil and cook until reduced by half, 6 to 7 minutes. Add the cream and cook until reduced by half, about 5 minutes. Add the tomato sauce and bring to a boil. Reduce the heat to low and keep warm while the pasta is cooking.

Bring 5 quarts of water and the salt to a boil in a large stockpot over high heat. Add the penne and cook until al dente. Transfer to a colander to drain. Add to the pan with the tomato-vodka sauce and toss to coat evenly. Transfer to a serving platter and sprinkle with the parmigiano and parsley.

3 tablespoons olive oil

9 ounces pancetta, sliced ¼ inch thick, unrolled into strips, and julienned

2 shallots, minced

1 cup vodka

1 ½ cups heavy whipping cream

1 cup Salsa di Pomodoro (page 24)

5 teaspoons sea salt

1 pound dry penne rigate

⅓ cup freshly grated Parmigiano–Reggiano

1 tablespoon chopped fresh Italian parsley

*Farfalle al Salmone*

◎

SERVES 6

3 tablespoons olive oil

2 tablespoons unsalted butter

2 shallots, minced

6 ounces sliced smoked salmon, julienned

1/3 cup capers, drained and chopped (see Note)

1 tablespoon chopped fresh dill or wild fennel

1/2 teaspoon freshly ground pepper

1/2 cup brandy

1 1/2 cups heavy whipping cream

1 cup Salsa di Pomodoro (page 24)

5 1/2 teaspoons sea salt

1 pound dry farfalle

One of Italy's few landlocked regions, Trentino–Alto Adige relies on freshwater fish harvested from its many lakes and saltwater fish that have been smoked or cured, like the smoked salmon in this recipe.

Heat the olive oil and butter in a large sauté pan over medium-high heat until the butter melts. Add the shallots and cook 2 to 3 minutes. Add the salmon, capers, half the dill, and 1/4 teaspoon of the pepper. Remove from the heat, add the brandy, and light with a match. Return to the heat and carefully swirl the pan to mix the ingredients and burn off the alcohol. Continue cooking until the liquid has completely evaporated, 2 to 3 minutes. Add the cream, bring to a boil, and cook until reduced by half, about 5 minutes. Add the tomato sauce and bring to a boil. Cook 5 to 10 minutes more.

Bring 5 quarts of water and 5 teaspoons of the salt to a boil in a large stockpot over high heat. Add the farfalle and cook until al dente. Transfer to a colander to drain. Add to the pan with the smoked salmon sauce. Add the remaining 1/2 teaspoon of salt and 1/4 teaspoon of pepper. Stir to mix well. Transfer to a serving platter and sprinkle with the remaining dill.

Note: To chop the capers, place them on a cutting board and, using the side of a chef's knife, gently smash them before chopping. This releases their flavor and prevents them from rolling off the cutting board.

# Spinach Dumplings with a Ham and Cream Sauce
## Spätzle Crema e Speck

◉

**For the spätzle:**

2 tablespoons olive oil

2 tablespoons finely diced onion

5 ounces baby spinach leaves

3/4 cup freshly grated Parmigiano-Reggiano

1 large egg, beaten

1/2 teaspoon sea salt

1/4 teaspoon freshly ground pepper

1 cup all-purpose flour

**For the sauce:**

2 tablespoons unsalted butter

1/4 pound speck or smoked ham, julienned

1/2 cup dry white wine

1/4 teaspoon freshly ground pepper

1 1/2 cups heavy whipping cream

1/2 cup freshly grated Parmigiano-Reggiano

5 teaspoons sea salt

2 tablespoons chopped fresh Italian parsley

Alto Adige is best known for speck, a smoked ham flavored with juniper, garlic, pepper, and herbs. Prepared according to family tradition, it varies slightly from home to home. It is wildly popular, regardless of whether it is consumed as a snack, a lunch dish, or as an ingredient in a pasta sauce. I've included it in this German-inspired spätzle recipe. Speck can usually be found at Italian specialty stores; if you aren't able to locate it, smoked ham is a fine substitute.

To make the spätzle: Heat the olive oil in a large sauté pan over medium-high heat. Add the onion and cook until soft, about 3 minutes. Add the spinach and cook until completely tender, about 5 minutes. Transfer to a colander to let cool. Squeeze between your hands to eliminate any excess liquid from the spinach. Transfer to the bowl of a food processor and chop until a fine mixture is achieved. Transfer to a medium bowl. Add the parmigiano, egg, salt, and pepper. Mix well. Add the flour and mix until completely combined. Shape into a ball and let sit 10 to 15 minutes.

Roll the dough into a cylinder 2 to 2 1/2 inches in diameter. Cut into 1-inch-thick slices. Working with one slice at a time, set it on its edge and then press it down to flatten it. Place on a flat work surface and roll each slice into a cylinder 3/4 inch in diameter. As you roll, spread your fingers out to create a long, even roll. Dust generously with flour and cut into 1/4-inch-thick slices. Shape the spätzle as directed on page 23.

To make the sauce: Melt the butter in a large sauté pan over medium-high heat. Add the speck and cook until crispy, 5 to 7 minutes. Add the wine and pepper and increase the heat to high. Cook until the wine is nearly evaporated, about 5 minutes. Add the cream and 1/4 cup of the parmigiano; bring to a boil and cook until reduced by a quarter, about 3 minutes.

Bring 5 quarts of water and the 5 teaspoons of salt to a boil over high heat. Add the spätzle and boil until cooked through, about 3 minutes. Transfer to a colander to drain. Add to the pan with the cream sauce and add the remaining 1/4 cup of parmigiano; toss to coat evenly. Serve sprinkled with the parsley.

*Canederli Tirolesi*

---

SERVES 6

The cuisine of Trentino-Alto Adige, the northernmost region of Italy, is heavily influenced by both Austria, which it borders, and Germany. These rich dumplings, called canederli, were adopted from those countries and transformed by Adige's innovative cooks to become an Italian favorite.

To make the spinach dumplings: Place the bread in a bowl and cover with the milk. Let sit 15 minutes. Drain and squeeze out any excess milk. Transfer the bread to the bowl of a food processor and chop until a fine mixture is achieved. Transfer to a medium bowl.

Heat the olive oil in a large sauté pan over medium-high heat. Add the garlic and cook 1 minute. Add the spinach and cook until completely tender, 5 to 10 minutes. Transfer to a colander to drain. Let cool. Squeeze the spinach between your hands to eliminate any excess liquid. Transfer to the bowl of a food processor and chop until a fine mixture is achieved. Add to the bowl with the bread. Add the eggs and mix well. Add the parmigiano, salt, and pepper. Mix well. Set aside.

To make the mushroom dumplings: Place the porcini in a small bowl. Add the hot water and let sit 30 minutes. Place the bread in a bowl and cover with the milk. Let sit 15 minutes. Drain and squeeze out any excess milk. Transfer the bread to the bowl of a food processor and chop until a fine mixture is achieved. Transfer to a medium bowl.

Remove the porcini from the water with your hands. Transfer to a colander to drain. Strain the liquid to remove any sand and reserve. Squeeze the porcini to eliminate any excess liquid. Chop into a fine dice.

Heat the olive oil in a large sauté pan over medium-high heat. Add the garlic and cook 1 minute. Remove the garlic. Add the porcini, button, shiitake, and cremini mushrooms and cook until crispy, 7 to 10 minutes. Add the wine and cook until nearly evaporated, about 3 minutes. Add the reserved liquid from the porcini and cook until completely evaporated, about 5 minutes. (The mushrooms need to be dry.) Transfer the mushrooms to the bowl with the bread crumbs, using a slotted spoon. Add the eggs and mix well. Add the parmigiano, a pinch of salt, and pepper. Mix well. Set aside.

To make the ricotta-pancetta dumplings: Place the bread in a bowl and cover with the milk. Let sit 15 minutes. Drain and squeeze out any excess milk. Transfer the bread to the bowl of a food processor and chop until a fine mixture is achieved. Transfer to a medium bowl.

(continued on next page)

---

*For the spinach dumplings:*

5 cups (about ¾ pound) fresh bread cubes (see Note on next page)

½ cup milk

¼ cup olive oil

3 garlic cloves, smashed

10 ounces baby spinach leaves

2 large eggs, beaten

½ cup freshly grated Parmigiano-Reggiano

½ teaspoon sea salt

½ teaspoon freshly ground pepper

*For the mushroom dumplings:*

½ ounce dried porcini mushrooms

¾ cup hot water

5 cups (about ¾ pound) fresh bread cubes (see Note on next page)

½ cup milk

¼ cup olive oil

1 garlic clove, smashed

2 medium button mushrooms, stemmed and finely diced

2 medium shiitake mushrooms, stemmed and finely diced

*(ingredients continued on next page)*

*(ingredients continued from previous page)*

*2 medium cremini mushrooms, stemmed and finely diced*

*½ cup dry white wine*

*2 large eggs, beaten*

*¾ cup freshly grated Parmigiano-Reggiano*

*Sea salt*

*Freshly ground pepper*

*For the ricotta-pancetta dumplings:*

*3½ cups (about ½ pound) fresh bread cubes (see Note)*

*½ cup milk*

*5 ounces pancetta, finely diced*

*2 large eggs, beaten*

*1 cup ricotta cheese*

*¾ cup freshly grated Parmigiano-Reggiano, plus extra for serving*

*1 tablespoon chopped fresh chives*

*½ teaspoon sea salt*

*½ teaspoon freshly ground pepper*

*4 quarts chicken stock*

Heat a large sauté pan over medium-high heat and add the pancetta. Cook until crispy, about 5 minutes, being careful not to burn the pancetta. Drain the pancetta to remove the oil, and add to the bowl with the bread. Add the eggs and mix well. Add the ricotta, parmigiano, chives, salt, and pepper. Mix well. Set aside.

To assemble the dish: Divide each of the three canederli mixtures into 6 portions (about 4 ounces each). Roll each portion into a firm ball, using your hands.

Bring the chicken stock to a boil in a large stockpot over medium-high heat. Add the canederli and cook until heated through, 10 to 15 minutes. For each serving, arrange one of each type of canederli in a bowl and ladle stock over the top. Serve with additional parmigiano.

Note: A soft white bread is easy to work with in this recipe, but stale bread can always be used.

# Potato Ravioli Filled with Spinach and Sausage and Topped with Brown Butter and Sage

*Offelle alla Triestina*

◎

SERVES 6

**For the pasta:**

2 medium baking potatoes
(about ¾ pound each)

1 ¼ cups
all-purpose flour

2 teaspoons active
dry yeast

½ teaspoon sea salt

1 large egg

**For the filling:**

3 tablespoons olive oil

¾ pound mild Italian
sausage, crumbled

1 cup dry red wine

¼ medium onion, diced

2 garlic cloves, smashed

10 ounces baby
spinach leaves

¾ cup freshly grated
Parmigiano-Reggiano

Sea salt

Freshly ground pepper

1 egg, beaten

6 cups chicken stock

½ cup (1 stick)
unsalted butter

12 fresh sage leaves

Sea salt

½ cup freshly grated
Parmigiano-Reggiano

*In Italy, potatoes are often used as an ingredient for pasta dough. The trick to making light, airy potato pasta is to bake the potatoes to remove all of their moisture. In this recipe, a robust-flavored potato dough is stuffed with a flavorful filling and topped with a buttery herb sauce, resulting in a dish full of personality.*

To make the pasta dough: Preheat the oven to 450°F. Wrap the potatoes in a double layer of aluminum foil and place in an ovenproof skillet. Bake until tender, about 1 hour and 30 minutes. Let cool.

Peel the potatoes and press through a potato ricer onto a flat work surface. Combine the flour, yeast, and salt in a small bowl. Sprinkle over the potato. Beat the egg with a fork in a small bowl. Pour over the potato. Mix together, using your hands. Continue mixing with your hands, scraping with a spatula to loosen any dough that sticks to the surface as you mix and adding flour as needed, until the dough no longer sticks to your hands. Gently knead the pasta dough until it is completely smooth. (This dough will remain soft because of the potatoes.) Shape the pasta into a ball, cover with plastic wrap, and let rest at least 30 minutes in the refrigerator.

To make the filling: Heat 1 tablespoon of the olive oil in a large sauté pan over medium-high heat. Add the sausage and cook until crispy, about 10 minutes. Drain the excess fat from the sauté pan and return to the heat. Add the wine and cook until nearly evaporated, about 5 minutes. Transfer the sausage to the bowl of a food processor. Wipe out the sauté pan and return it to the stove.

Heat the remaining 2 tablespoons of olive oil over medium-high heat. Add the onion and garlic and cook until soft, about 5 minutes. Add the spinach, reduce the heat to medium, and cook until tender, about 10 minutes. Transfer to a colander to cool. Squeeze the spinach between your hands to eliminate any excess liquid. Transfer to the food processor with the sausage. Pulse until a coarse mixture is achieved. Add the parmigiano, season with salt and pepper, and pulse just to combine.

Roll the pasta out to a $1/2$-inch-thick disk, using a rolling pin. Divide into 4 portions. On a flat, floured work surface, roll out one portion to a $1/8$-inch-thick rectangle about 4 inches wide by 18 inches long, dusting with flour as needed. Cut the pasta in half lengthwise, forming 2 long strips. Brush one strip with some of the beaten egg. Pipe out (or drop by the spoonful) 12 small mounds (about 1 teaspoon each) of the filling, spacing them about 2 inches apart. Arrange the other strip of pasta over the filling and gently push the pasta down around each mound to push out any air. Cut into 2-inch squares. Transfer the pasta to a flour-dusted platter. Repeat this procedure with the remaining pasta and filling.

Bring the chicken stock to a boil in a large stockpot over medium-high heat. Gently add the offelle and cook until the pasta is firm when pressed with your fingertip, 8 to 10 minutes. Transfer to a colander to drain, and then transfer to a serving platter.

Melt the butter in a large sauté pan over medium-high heat. Add the sage and 2 pinches of salt. Cook until the sage is crispy and the butter begins to brown, about 5 minutes. Sprinkle the parmigiano over the offelle. Pour the butter and sage over the pasta and serve while the butter is still bubbling.

# SAUTÉED PRAWNS WITH CAPERS, CREAM, AND TOMATO SAUCE OVER THIN PASTA STRANDS

*Vermicelli alla Busara*

SERVES 6

The name for this dish, busara, *derives from the name of a covered container once favored by sailors for transporting this pasta. The primary flavors are the prawns (which must be the largest you can buy) and the capers. The best capers are from Pantelleria, a small island south of Sicilia. They are cured in salt and are more flavorful than capers brined in liquid.*

Set the prawns on a cutting board, shell-side up. Make an insertion in the middle of the head with a sharp chef's knife and cut the body in half, lengthwise. Set aside.

Heat the olive oil in a large sauté pan over high heat. Dredge the meat of the prawns in the flour and place in the sauté pan, floured-side down. Cook until browned and crispy, about 5 minutes. Turn, and add the garlic, peperoncini, and capers. Remove from the heat, add the brandy, and light with a match. Return to the heat and carefully swirl the pan to mix the ingredients and burn off the alcohol. Add the wine when the flame is extinguished. Cook until all of the liquid is nearly evaporated, about 5 minutes. Add the tomato sauce and cream. Bring to a boil. Remove the prawns and set aside. The prawns should be slightly undercooked. Do not overcook or they will become tough and chewy. Cook the sauce until thick, 5 to 8 minutes.

Bring 5 quarts of water and the salt to a boil in a large stockpot over high heat. Add the pasta and cook until al dente. Transfer to a colander to drain. Add the pasta to the sauté pan and cook 2 minutes. The starch from the pasta will act as a thickener for the sauce. Drizzle with the extra-virgin olive oil and sprinkle with the pepper. Divide the pasta among 6 plates and top each serving with a prawn.

## Pasta Etiquette

As a matter of form and function, cutting pasta is frowned upon. This prohibition may be connected with the history of the fork, which was invented in Italy. Originally only the upper classes had forks, and the lower classes used their hands to eat pasta. Most likely, as the fork gained widespread use, the upper classes distinguished themselves by only twirling and never cutting. Today, twirling pasta is more a question of taste than of social class. It's the best way to catch the sauce. To twirl pasta properly, long strands should be caught between the tines of a fork and then twisted around until neatly wrapped. It may take some practice, but it is the most authentic way to eat pasta. Or, you can rest the tines of the fork against the bowl of a soup-spoon, to more easily twirl the pasta.

6 large prawns, heads and tails intact

1 cup olive oil

Flour for dredging

4 garlic cloves, chopped

2 small dried peperoncini, broken into small pieces

¼ cup capers, drained and chopped (see Note on page 54)

¼ cup brandy

½ cup dry white wine

1 tablespoon chopped fresh Italian parsley

2 cups Salsa di Pomodoro (page 24)

1 cup heavy whipping cream

5 teaspoons sea salt

1 pound dry vermicelli

2 tablespoons extra-virgin olive oil

¼ teaspoon freshly ground pepper

# BEET-FLAVORED PASTA STUFFED WITH A RICOTTA-BEET FILLING TOPPED WITH BROWN BUTTER AND POPPY SEEDS

*Casonsei Ampezzani*

SERVES 6

*For the pasta:*

½ cup chopped
cooked beet (about
½ of a large beet)

1⅔ cups
all-purpose flour

½ teaspoon sea salt

1 large egg at room
temperature

*For the filling:*

One 15-ounce
container ricotta

⅓ cup finely diced
cooked beet

¼ cup toasted
bread crumbs

½ teaspoon sea salt

¼ teaspoon freshly
ground pepper

¼ teaspoon freshly
grated nutmeg

1 egg, beaten

5 teaspoons sea salt

½ cup (1 stick)
unsalted butter

½ cup freshly grated
Parmigiano-Reggiano

1 tablespoon poppy seeds

Cortina, the Aspen of Italy, is one of my favorite places to ski. Once, while on a trip with friends, it was suggested that we visit a restaurant renowned for its pasta. We drove for many hours, only to find an old barn in the middle of nowhere. We were pleasantly surprised by the large table in the center of the room, which displayed the most incredible selection of fresh pasta. We selected the pasta we wanted, and the servers carried it to the kitchen to be cooked. That was the first time I tasted this particular dish, and it has since become a favorite.

To make the pasta: Purée the beet in the bowl of a food processor or in a food mill. Combine the flour and salt on a flat work surface or in a wide, shallow bowl and shape into a mound. Make a well in the center and add the egg. Beat the egg with a fork. Add the beet purée to the egg and gradually begin beating in a wider path to incorporate the flour. Continue mixing with the fork until the pasta begins to resemble a dry, crumbly mixture. Transfer to a flat work surface dusted with flour. Begin kneading by hand, rolling the dough sideways across the surface from hand to hand, and applying strong pressure while squeezing the dough. Knead until all of the flour is incorporated, no floury white spots remain, and the pasta begins to soften, about 10 minutes. Shape into a ball, cover with plastic wrap, and let sit 30 minutes. (This allows the flour to continue to absorb moisture from the liquid.)

To make the filling: Combine the ricotta, beet, bread crumbs, salt, pepper, and nutmeg in a medium bowl. Mix well. Transfer to a large pastry bag with a 1-inch opening.

Roll out the pasta as described in steps 1 and 2 under "To roll out sheets" on page 22. Brush one long half of a pasta sheet with some of the beaten egg. Pipe out (or drop by the spoonful) 9 small mounds (about 1 tablespoon each) of the filling, spacing them about 2½ inches apart on top of the egg-brushed side. Fold the other pasta half over, forming a long rectangle, and gently push the pasta down around each mound to push out any air. Arrange a 2½-inch fluted cookie cutter around the edge of each mound and press down to cut into half-moon shapes. Transfer to a platter dusted with flour. Repeat with the remaining pasta and filling.

Bring 5 quarts of water and the 5 teaspoons of salt to a boil in a large stockpot over high heat. Add the casonsei and cook until they rise to the top, about 2 minutes. Transfer to a colander.

Melt 6 tablespoons of the butter in a large sauté pan over medium-high heat. Add the casonsei. Cook until crisp, turn, and cook the other side, about 2 minutes per side. Transfer to a platter and sprinkle with the parmigiano. Melt the remaining 2 tablespoons of butter in the sauté pan over medium-high heat and cook until browned. Spoon over the casonsei. Sprinkle with the poppy seeds.

◎

SERVES 6

One 28-ounce can
whole peeled tomatoes
with their juice

½ cup olive oil

½ medium onion, sliced

4 garlic cloves, sliced

2 medium dried
peperoncini, broken
into small pieces

One 2-ounce tin
anchovy fillets, drained
and coarsely chopped

2 tablespoons chopped
fresh Italian parsley

5 teaspoons sea salt,
plus extra for seasoning

Freshly ground pepper

1 pound dry spaghettini

½ cup freshly grated
Parmigiano-Reggiano

2 tablespoons chopped
fresh Italian parsley

2 tablespoons
extra-virgin olive oil

This is a variation of bigoli in salsa, a dish well loved in Venice, where the bigoli noodle—a long strand with a hollow center to catch the sauce—was invented. This version is from Treviso. My mother prepared it to please my father, who was raised there. She made the dish on Good Friday every year.

Put the tomatoes in a medium bowl and break up with your hands. Set aside. Heat the olive oil in a large sauté pan over medium-high heat. Add the onion, garlic, and peperoncini. Cook 1 minute. Add the anchovies, parsley, and a pinch of salt and pepper. Cook until the onion is tender, about 5 minutes. Add the tomatoes to the pan and bring to a boil. Reduce the heat and simmer 30 minutes. Season with salt.

Bring 5 quarts of water and the 5 teaspoons of salt to a boil in a large stockpot over high heat. Add the pasta and cook until al dente. Transfer to a colander to drain. Add to the pan with the anchovy-tomato sauce and toss to coat evenly. Transfer to a serving dish. Sprinkle with the parmigiano and parsley. Drizzle with the extra-virgin olive oil.

# SEAFOOD BAKED IN A TOMATO SAUCE WITH ROUND PASTA STRANDS

*Bigoli in Casso Pipa*

---

SERVES 6

The name for this dish derives from its cooking vessel and method. Casso *is an older name used for* a clay pot, *and* pipa *means to "simmer something slowly." The dish makes for a dramatic presentation when brought to the table and uncovered, as the aroma is released and fills the air with this "Italian perfume."*

Preheat the oven to 400°F.

Heat a large sauté pan over high heat. Add the clams, mussels, parsley, and a pinch of pepper. Cover and cook until the clams and mussels begin to open, 1 to 2 minutes. Be careful not to overcook. Spread on a baking sheet to cool. Strain the liquid and reserve. Remove the clams and mussels from their shells by gently scraping with a small spoon. Discard the shells.

Heat the olive oil in a large sauté pan over medium-high heat. Add the garlic and cook for 1 minute. Add the shrimp and scallops. Cook until the shrimp begin to turn bright orange, 2 to 3 minutes. Add the clams, mussels, anchovies, and crab. Add the brandy and light with a match. Return to the heat and carefully swirl the pan to mix the ingredients and burn off the alcohol. Add the reserved cooking liquid from the clams and mussels and bring to a boil. Cook until reduced by half. Transfer to the bowl of a food processor and pulse while counting 1-2-3, and stop. Do not overprocess.

Bake the empty clay pot in the oven until hot, about 10 minutes. Add the seafood mixture and tomato sauce. Cover and bake until the mixture begins to boil, about 5 minutes. Reduce the heat to 350°F and bake until a thin layer of oil begins to appear on the top, about 30 minutes.

Bring 5 quarts of water and the salt to a boil in a large stockpot over high heat. Add the pasta and cook until not quite al dente, a few minutes less than the package directions suggest. Transfer to a colander to drain. Add to the seafood mixture, cover, and bake until the flavors meld, about 3 minutes. Bring to the table and serve from the clay pot.

1 pound small, fresh clams, well rinsed (see Note on page 72)

1 pound mussels, well rinsed and debearded

1 ½ teaspoons chopped fresh Italian parsley

Freshly ground pepper

½ cup olive oil

3 garlic cloves, smashed

2 ounces shrimp, peeled, deveined, and chopped

2 ounces scallops, cut into ¼-inch-thick slices

One 2-ounce tin anchovy fillets

2 ounces lump crabmeat

¼ cup brandy

2 cups Salsa di Pomodoro (page 24)

5 teaspoons sea salt

1 pound dry bigoli

# FRESH PASTA BAKED IN A CREAMY SEAFOOD SAUCE
## *Pasticcio di Pesce*

◎

SERVES 6

The name for this dish, pasticcio, *means "trouble" or "imperfect." When the lasagne is cut and transferred to a plate, it spreads out and makes a tiny mess. This is an unusual pasta dish in that it improves from sitting, and therefore can be assembled up to one day in advance of cooking.*

Prepare the pasta as directed on page 21. Let sit 30 minutes.

To cook the mussels and clams: Heat the olive oil in a large, high-sided sauté pan over high heat. Add the mussels, clams, parsley, and garlic. Quickly squeeze the lemon over the mussels and clams, then add it to the pan and cover. Cook until the mussels and clams begin to open, 1 to 2 minutes. Be careful not to overcook. Spread on a baking sheet to cool. Strain the liquid into a medium bowl and reserve. Remove the mussels and clams from their shells by gently scraping with a small spoon. Discard the shells.

To make the béchamel sauce: Slowly bring the milk to a low boil in a medium saucepan over medium-low heat. Melt the butter in a large saucepan over medium heat. Add the flour to the butter and cook, stirring, until the flour is well incorporated, about 2 minutes. Whisk in the milk, nutmeg, salt, and white pepper. Mix well. Whisk in the reserved liquid from the mussels and clams and bring to a boil. Cook until the mixture becomes thick, about 10 minutes. Remove from the heat. Drizzle a small amount of olive oil over the top of the sauce to prevent a skin from forming.

To make the filling: Heat the olive oil in a large sauté pan over high heat. Add the garlic and cook 1 minute. Add the shrimp, scallops, peperoncino, bay leaf, and pepper. Cook 1 minute. Remove from the heat, add the brandy, and light with a match. Return to the heat and carefully swirl the pan to mix the ingredients and burn off the alcohol. Add the wine when the flame is extinguished. Cook 1 minute. Stir in the clams and mussels. Add the béchamel and bring to a boil. Add the crabmeat and remove from the heat.

Roll out the pasta as described in steps 1 and 2 under "To roll out sheets" on page 22. Cut each 24-inch sheet crosswise into two 12-inch lasagne noodles, for a total of 4.

Preheat the oven to 450°F.

Bring 5 quarts of water and the salt to a boil over medium-high heat. Add a splash of olive oil and 2 lasagne noodles. Cook 2 to 3 minutes, stirring to prevent sticking. Transfer to a colander to drain. Line a cutting board with plastic wrap and set a lasagne noodle on the plastic. Cover with another sheet of plastic wrap to prevent sticking, and top with the second noodle, then cover with plastic. Cook the remaining 2 noodles and layer between sheets of plastic.

(continued on next page)

1 recipe Basic Pasta
*(page 21)*

*For the mussels and clams:*

¼ *cup olive oil*

1 ½ *pounds mussels, well rinsed and debearded*

1 ½ *pounds small, fresh clams, well rinsed (see Note on next page)*

1 ½ *teaspoons chopped fresh Italian parsley*

3 *large garlic cloves, smashed*

½ *lemon*

*For the béchamel sauce:*

2 ½ *cups milk*

5 *tablespoons unsalted butter*

½ *cup all-purpose flour*

¼ *teaspoon freshly grated nutmeg*

½ *teaspoon sea salt*

½ *teaspoon freshly ground white pepper*

*Olive oil for drizzling*

*For the filling:*

⅓ *cup olive oil*

3 *garlic cloves, chopped*

¼ *pound medium shrimp, peeled and deveined*

*(ingredients continued on next page)*

*(ingredients continued from previous page)*

¼ *pound sea scallops, cut into ¼-inch-thick slices*

½ *small dried peperoncino, broken into small pieces*

1 *fresh bay leaf*

¼ *teaspoon freshly ground black pepper*

¼ *cup brandy*

½ *cup dry white wine*

¼ *pound fresh lump crabmeat*

5 *teaspoons sea salt*

*Olive oil*

2 *tablespoons chopped fresh Italian parsley*

Drizzle a small amount of olive oil in the bottom of a 12-by-6-by-3-inch oval baking dish. Cut the pasta to fit the baking dish, using a pastry cutter. Spread a small portion of the seafood sauce in the bottom of the dish and arrange a pasta sheet over the sauce. Sprinkle with a third of the parsley. Repeat the layers until all of the ingredients have been used, finishing with the sauce as the top layer. Drizzle with 1 tablespoon of olive oil. Bake until heated through, about 20 minutes. Remove from the oven and push the lasagne away from the sides with a spatula. Sprinkle with additional parsley. Let rest 2 to 3 minutes before cutting into serving-size portions.

Note: I prefer to use Manila or New Zealand clams because they are the most readily available on the West Coast. You can use any local fresh clams, but avoid the larger ones, which can be tough.

*Handling Hot Pasta*

Cooking larger noodles, such as cannelloni or lasagne, requires patience. First, the noodles should be cooked only 2 at a time to prevent them from sticking to each other. Once they have finished cooking, they require gentle handling to prevent tearing. Before removing hot pasta sheets from a colander, one trick is to rinse your fingers under cold water. The cold will temporarily stave off the heat of the pasta, and make handling the hot noodles manageable.

# EGGPLANT-POTATO DUMPLINGS
## TOPPED WITH A TOMATO-BASIL SAUCE
### Gnocchi alle Melanzane

SERVES 6

Baking the eggplant until the moisture evaporates concentrates the flavor and results in a robust and tender bite of gnocchi.

Preheat the oven to 450°F.

Place the eggplants, scored-side down, in a colander. Sprinkle with 1/2 teaspoon of the salt and let sit 1 hour.

Wrap the potatoes in a double layer of aluminum foil and place in an ovenproof skillet. Bake until tender, about 1 hour and 30 minutes. Let cool.

Pat the eggplant dry with paper towels. Rub olive oil over the top of each eggplant half (use about 1 tablespoon all together) and sprinkle with 1/4 teaspoon of the salt. Bake until tender, about 45 minutes. Remove most of the seeds. Spoon the pulp from the skin and transfer to a baking sheet. Bake until all of the moisture evaporates, 10 to 15 minutes. Transfer to the bowl of a food processor and purée.

Peel the potatoes and press through a potato ricer onto a flat work surface. Add the eggplant and 1/4 cup of the flour and mix well. Beat the egg with a fork in a small bowl. Pour over the potato mixture. Mix together, using your hands, scraping with a spatula to loosen any dough that sticks to the surface as you mix and adding flour as needed, until the dough no longer sticks to your hands. Gently knead the pasta until it is completely smooth. Wash your hands with hot water to eliminate any residual flour.

Roll the dough into a 5-inch-long cylinder, and then 5 longer cylinders, as directed in the Step-by-Step Guide for Shaping Dumplings on page 23. Cut into 3/4-inch pieces. Press each piece against the tines on the back of a fork while gently rolling it down. Transfer to a flour-dusted plate with a spatula.

Heat the remaining 1/4 cup of olive oil in a large sauté pan over medium-high heat. Add the garlic and cook 1 minute. Add the tomato and basil and cook 1 minute. Season with salt and pepper. Add the tomato sauce and bring to a boil. Reduce the heat to low and keep warm while the pasta is cooking.

Bring 5 quarts of water and the remaining 5 teaspoons of sea salt to a boil in a large stockpot over high heat. Add the gnocchi and cook until they rise to the top, about 5 minutes. Transfer to a colander to drain. Add to the pan with the tomato sauce and toss to coat evenly. Transfer to a serving dish and sprinkle with the parmigiano.

4 large eggplants (about 3/4 pound each), halved and meat side scored

5 3/4 teaspoons sea salt, plus extra for seasoning

2 medium baking potatoes (about 3/4 pound each)

1/4 cup plus 1 tablespoon olive oil

1/4 to 1/2 cup all-purpose flour

1 large egg

1 garlic clove, smashed

1 ripe large tomato, peeled, seeded, and finely diced

4 fresh medium basil leaves, torn into small pieces

Freshly ground pepper

2 cups Salsa di Pomodoro (page 24)

1/2 cup freshly grated Parmigiano-Reggiano

# RICOTTA-SPINACH DUMPLINGS
## BAKED IN A CREAMY PORCINI MUSHROOM SAUCE
### Boccon del Prete

◎

1 ounce dried
porcini mushrooms

1 cup hot water

½ cup olive oil

1 garlic clove, smashed

6 ounces baby
spinach leaves

2 ½ cups ricotta

1 ½ cups freshly grated
Parmigiano-Reggiano

5 ½ teaspoons sea salt

½ teaspoon freshly
ground pepper

¼ teaspoon freshly
grated nutmeg

1 large egg, beaten

1 ½ cups
all-purpose flour

1 small shallot, minced

1 tablespoon fresh
thyme leaves

½ cup dry white wine

2 cups heavy
whipping cream

It is rumored that this dish, which translates as "bite of the priest," was the creation of a woman who cooked and cleaned for a priest in the Veneto region. The dish is on the menu in our restaurant Canaletto Ristorante Veneto, a Venetian restaurant in Las Vegas's Venetian Hotel, and is a favorite of our customers at Il Fornaio as well.

Place the porcini in a small bowl. Cover with the hot water. Let sit 30 minutes.

Preheat the broiler.

Heat ¼ cup of the olive oil in a large sauté pan over medium-high heat. Add the garlic and cook 1 minute. Add the spinach and cook until tender, about 5 minutes. Transfer to a colander. Let cool. Squeeze the spinach between your hands to eliminate any excess liquid. Transfer to the bowl of a food processor and purée.

Combine the ricotta, 1 cup of the parmigiano, ¼ teaspoon of the salt, ¼ teaspoon of the pepper, and the nutmeg in a wide, shallow bowl. Add the egg and mix well. Add the spinach and flour; mix, using your hands.

Roll the dough into a 5-inch-long cylinder, and then 5 longer cylinders, as directed in the Step-by-Step Guide for Shaping Dumplings on page 23. Cut on the diagonal into ¼-inch-thick slices. Transfer to a flour-dusted plate with a spatula.

Heat the remaining ¼ cup of olive oil in a large sauté pan over medium-high heat. Add the shallot and cook until soft, 2 to 3 minutes. Remove the porcini from the water with your hands. Transfer to a colander to drain and discard the soaking liquid. Squeeze the porcini to eliminate any excess liquid. Chop and add to the sauté pan. Add the thyme and remaining ¼ tea-

spoon of pepper; cook 5 minutes. Add the wine and cook until the liquid is nearly evaporated, about 3 minutes. Add the cream and ¼ teaspoon of the salt; cook until the cream is reduced by a quarter, about 5 minutes.

Bring 5 quarts of water and the remaining 5 teaspoons of salt to a boil in a large stockpot over high heat. Add the gnocchi and cook until they rise to the top, about 5 minutes. Transfer to a colander to drain. Add to the pan with the mushroom sauce and toss to coat evenly. Transfer to a gratin or baking dish. Sprinkle with the remaining ½ cup of parmigiano and place under the broiler. Cook until browned, about 5 minutes.

### A Venetian Dream

When the Venetian, a grand hotel in Las Vegas, was being created in 1998, Il Fornaio was invited to design a restaurant for it. We joined forces with the Venetian and built Canaletto Ristorante Veneto, named for eighteenth-century Venetian painter Giovanni Antonio Canal, known as "Canaletto," who was famous for his paintings of Venice. His artwork is honored in the unique two-story setting of the restaurant. Opening Canaletto was like a dream come true for me, because I was able to share the culture of Venice with people through its food, including the dishes I love from my home.

## Rigatoni alla Crudaiola

4 small ripe tomatoes, peeled, seeded, and diced

½ cup olive oil

¼ medium onion, diced

2 garlic cloves, smashed

1 small dried peperoncino, broken into pieces

12 large cherry tomatoes, peeled and halved

5 ½ teaspoons sea salt, plus extra for seasoning

20 fresh medium basil leaves, torn into small pieces

½ cup kalamata olives, pitted and cut into wedges

¼ cup capers, drained and chopped (see Note on page 54)

One 2-ounce tin anchovy fillets, minced

2 tablespoons fresh oregano leaves, chopped

½ teaspoon freshly ground pepper

1 pound dry rigatoni

½ cup freshly grated Parmigiano-Reggiano

2 tablespoons extra-virgin olive oil

This was one of the most popular dishes at the restaurant in Venice where I learned to cook. All but the pasta was assembled in a ceramic bowl. The maitre d' then took the bowl to the table and added the pasta. After letting it sit, covered, for a moment, he removed the lid and released its aroma. The full flavor of this dish comes from fresh ingredients at the peak of their season, so it should only be prepared when you can get the best tomatoes and most vibrant basil.

Put the diced tomatoes in a colander to drain any excess liquid. Heat ¼ cup of the olive oil in a large sauté pan over medium-high heat. Add the onion, garlic, and peperoncino; cook until soft, 2 to 3 minutes. Add the cherry tomatoes and ½ teaspoon of the salt. Add half of the basil. Bring to a boil and cook 3 to 5 minutes. Transfer to the bowl of a food processor. Pulse to chop into a fine mixture without puréeing. Let cool.

Transfer the diced tomato in the colander to a large, decorative dish with a lid and add the cooked cherry tomato mixture. Add the remaining ¼ cup of olive oil. Add the remaining basil, the olives, capers, anchovies, oregano, and ¼ teaspoon of the pepper. Mix well and let sit to allow the flavors to meld. Season with salt.

Bring 5 quarts of water and the remaining 5 teaspoons of salt to a boil in a large stockpot over high heat. Add the rigatoni and cook until al dente. Drain well in a colander. Add to the tomato sauce and toss. Sprinkle with the parmigiano and remaining ¼ teaspoon of pepper. Drizzle with the extra-virgin olive oil.

# POTATO DUMPLINGS WITH CALAMARI AND RADICCHIO
*Gnocchetti con Calamari e Radicchio*

◉

SERVES 6

Radicchio, a member of the chicory family, is a native vegetable of Veneto. Its slightly bitter taste flavors many Venetian dishes. I prefer radicchio di Treviso, *the cone-shaped variety, because its large white veins make it less bitter than other types of radicchio. If it isn't available where you live, a round head of red radicchio can be substituted.*

Prepare the gnocchi dough and roll it into a 5-inch-long cylinder and then 5 longer cylinders, as directed in the Step-by-Step Guide for Shaping Dumplings on page 23. Cut into ½-inch pieces. Press each piece against the tines on the back of a fork while gently rolling it down. Transfer to a flour-dusted plate with a spatula.

Heat ½ cup of the olive oil in a large sauté pan over medium-high heat. Add the garlic, onion, anchovies, peperoncini, and parsley. Cook 1 to 2 minutes. Add the calamari and radicchio. Increase the heat to high and cook until all of the liquid is evaporated, about 5 minutes, stirring constantly. Add the wine and cook until nearly evaporated, 1 to 2 minutes. Add the diced tomatoes, puréed tomatoes, water, tomato paste, basil, and bay leaves. Cover, bring to a boil, reduce the heat, and simmer until the calamari are tender, 1 to 1½ hours. Remove from the heat and add the remaining ½ cup of olive oil. Season with salt and pepper.

Bring 5 quarts of water and the 5 teaspoons of salt to a boil in a large stockpot over high heat. Add the gnocchi and cook until they rise to the top, about 5 minutes. Transfer to a colander to drain. Add to the pan with the calamari sauce. Toss to mix well.

1 recipe Basic Gnocchi (page 23)

1 cup olive oil

4 garlic cloves, minced

½ medium onion, diced

6 anchovy fillets, chopped

1 ½ dried peperoncini, broken into small pieces

2 tablespoons chopped fresh Italian parsley

2 pounds cleaned calamari, chopped finely in a food processor

½ medium head Treviso radicchio, halved, cored, and shredded

1 cup dry white wine

2 cups peeled, seeded, diced tomato

1 cup canned whole peeled tomatoes with their juice, puréed

1 cup water

2 tablespoons tomato paste

6 fresh medium basil leaves, torn into small pieces

2 bay leaves

5 teaspoons sea salt, plus extra for seasoning

Freshly ground pepper

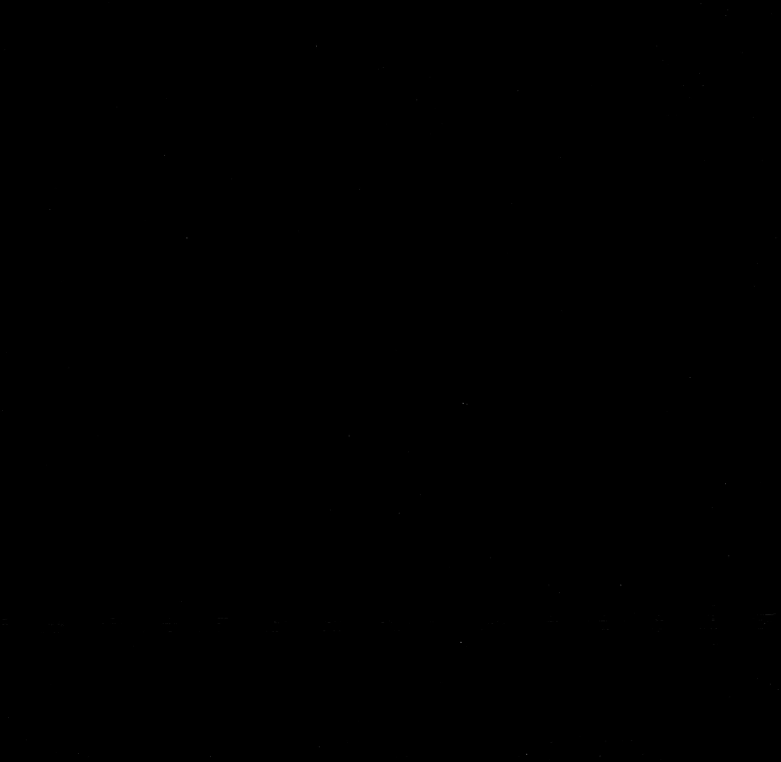

In the Heartland

When one thinks of Italy's heartland, it is easy to conjure up images of rolling hills, green fields, and rows of grapevines. A lot of the land is agricultural: this area has as many farmers as it does fishermen. Rivaling the regions to the north for culinary creations, the seven regions located in the center of the country—Emilia-Romagna, Toscana, Umbria, Marche, Lazio, Abruzzo, and Molise—are home to some of Italy's most beloved foods.

The land is used for raising both cattle and sheep. Among its most famous cow's milk cheeses is Emilia-Romagna's Parmigiano-Reggiano. Its lush, nutty, and salty essence is equalled only by the sheep's milk pecorino that is made in neighboring Lazio, Toscana, and Umbria. Sharp, slightly tangy, and yet milky-sweet, pecorino made from the sheep grazing in this countryside is distinctively different from southern versions.

The sausages and prosciutto made in the countryside are alone worthy of a trip to Italy. Every year, when we travel to Italy on my Chef's Tour, we visit a salumeria, or "sausage shop," in Siena. We make a lunch out of the delicious handmade sausages and cured meats that give so many of the region's pasta dishes a rich and unique flavor. If you are ever in Siena, please say hello to my friend Antonio at Antica Pizzicheria and enjoy some of Toscana's best sausages.

Tomatoes and artichokes are among the many vegetables that the heartland's cooks rely on to season their dishes. They are essential to the area's most famous pasta dishes, including the tomato sauces that are the signature of Lazio. As for Umbria's earthy and fragrant black truffle, it is a revered ingredient in whatever dish it graces.

Here, too, fresh pasta reigns. Tagliatelle from Emilia-Romagna, pici and pappardelle from Toscana, and fettuccine from Lazio are among the most popular fresh pastas of the area. In fact, according to tradition in Emilia-Romagna, the woman who made the best pasta would catch the best husband. Maybe that's why so many fresh pastas, stuffed, layered, and nestled in savory sauces, emerged from this region!

Time-honored recipes for the fresh and dry pasta dishes from these regions are included in this chapter. With each bite, you will have the opportunity to taste the area's most classic ingredients.

## EMILIA-ROMAGNA

*Tagliatelle alla Bolognese* 85
FRESH SPINACH PASTA RIBBONS
WITH A CLASSIC MEAT RAGÙ

*Garganelli ai Porcini e Parmigiano* 87
FRESH PASTA TUBES WITH PORCINI
MUSHROOMS AND PARMESAN

*Cappellacci alla Zucca* 88
BUTTERNUT SQUASH PASTA FILLED
WITH A BUTTERNUT SQUASH,
PARMESAN, AND WALNUT FILLING

*Rotolino di Pasta all'Emiliana* 90
HAM AND RICOTTA ROLLED IN
A SHEET OF PASTA AND
BAKED IN BÉCHAMEL SAUCE

## TOSCANA

*Crespelle alla Fiorentina* 93
DELICATE FRESH CRÊPES WITH
A SPINACH-RICOTTA FILLING

*Fusilli al Sugo di Olive* 94
CORKSCREW PASTA WITH A
SAUCE OF ASSORTED OLIVES
AND FRESH TOMATOES

*Pici con Salsiccia* 95
FRESH HAND-TWISTED NOODLES
TOPPED WITH A SAUSAGE SAUCE

*Pappardelle sull'Anatra* 97
WIDE PASTA RIBBONS
IN A DUCK SAUCE

*Spaghettini al Granchio* 98
FRESH CRAB WITH TOMATOES
AND THIN PASTA STRANDS

## UMBRIA

*Tagliatelle alle Fave* 100
PASTA RIBBONS WITH FAVA BEANS,
PECORINO, AND AGED RICOTTA

*Spaghetti alla Norcina* 103
PASTA STRANDS WITH
BLACK TRUFFLE SAUCE

## MARCHE

*Spaghetti alle Cozze* 105
MUSSELS, ANCHOVIES,
AND TOMATOES TOSSED WITH
PASTA STRANDS

## LAZIO

*Bucatini alla Carbonara* 107
HOLLOW, ROUND PASTA
STRANDS IN A CLASSIC SAUCE
OF PANCETTA AND EGGS

*Fusilli al Tonno* 108
CORKSCREW PASTA TOSSED
WITH A TUNA SAUCE

*Spaghetti Aglio, Olio e Peperoncino* 110
PASTA STRANDS WITH GARLIC,
OLIVE OIL, AND DRIED RED PEPPER

*Penne all'Arrabbiata* 111
A FIERY TOMATO SAUCE
WITH SMALL PASTA TUBES

*Perciatelli all'Amatriciana* 112
LONG, HOLLOW STRANDS IN
TOMATO AND PANCETTA SAUCE

*Cavatappi Tonno e Carciofi* 114
CORKSCREW-SHAPED PASTA WITH TUNA,
ARTICHOKES, AND TOMATO SAUCE

## ABRUZZO E MOLISE

*Vermicelli con Gamberi ai Fiori di Zucchine* 115
THIN PASTA STRANDS WITH
SHRIMP AND SQUASH BLOSSOMS

*Conchiglie con Rucola alla Molisana* 116
PASTA SHELLS WITH ARUGULA AND TOMATOES

*Chitarrine al Sugo d'Agnello* 117
PASTA STRANDS WITH A LAMB SAUCE

# FRESH SPINACH PASTA RIBBONS WITH A CLASSIC MEAT RAGÙ
## *Tagliatelle alla Bolognese*

---

*There is much debate over the origins of the famous sauce in this dish, ragù alla Bolognese. Some argue that it was the result of combining portions of leftover meat, others say it was created by peasants to stretch the meat further by adding vegetables. My version of this sauce is prepared using a combination of ground meats for greater complexity, rather than just beef and the traditional salt pork. The Italian word ragù is most likely from the French word for stew, ragoût, yet another possible explanation for the origin of the sauce.*

**For the pasta:**

6 ounces baby spinach leaves

1 ¼ cups all-purpose flour

1 large egg

1 teaspoon olive oil

1 teaspoon sea salt

**For the sauce:**

⅓ pound ground pork

⅓ pound ground beef chuck

3 ounces pancetta, finely chopped in a food processor

3 tablespoons olive oil

¼ teaspoon sea salt

½ cup dry red wine

½ medium onion, finely diced

½ celery stalk, finely diced

½ medium carrot, finely diced

2 teaspoons chopped fresh rosemary

2 teaspoons chopped fresh sage

1 garlic clove, smashed

1 fresh bay leaf

*(ingredients continued on next page)*

To make the pasta: Bring 2 quarts of water to a boil in a large stockpot. Add the spinach and cook until wilted, 4 to 5 minutes. Transfer to a colander to drain. Let cool. Squeeze the spinach between your hands to eliminate any excess liquid. Transfer to the bowl of a food processor and purée.

Arrange the flour in a mound on a flat work surface or in a wide, shallow bowl. Beat the egg, olive oil, and salt together in a medium bowl. Add the spinach and mix well. Make a well in the center of the flour and pour the spinach mixture into the well. Beat with a fork, gradually beating a wider path and incorporating the flour in very small amounts. Continue mixing with the fork until the pasta begins to resemble a dry, crumbly mixture. Transfer to a flat work surface dusted with flour. Begin kneading by hand, rolling the dough sideways across the surface from hand to hand, and applying strong pressure while squeezing the dough. Knead until all of the flour is incorporated, no floury white spots remain, and the pasta begins to soften, 5 to 10 minutes. Shape into a ball, cover with plastic wrap, and let sit 30 minutes. (This allows the flour to continue to absorb moisture.)

Roll out the pasta dough into two 48-inch sheets, as described in steps 1 to 6 under "To roll out strands and ribbons" on page 22. Cut each 48-inch sheet crosswise into 12-inch lengths. Using the pasta maker attachment, cut into tagliatelle-size noodles, ⅜ inch wide and 12 inches long. Transfer to a flour-dusted platter and sprinkle with additional flour. Let dry at least 2 hours, moving the pasta around occasionally to prevent sticking.

To make the sauce: Preheat the oven to 450°F.

Combine the pork, beef, pancetta, 1 tablespoon of the olive oil, and the salt in a large baking pan. Mix well and spread out in the pan. Bake 5 to 10 minutes until crispy and browned, stirring once. Add the wine and bake until evaporated, about 5 minutes.

*(continued on next page)*

*(ingredients continued from previous page)*

*1 ¼ cups water*

*1 large ripe tomato, peeled, seeded, and diced*

*2 tablespoons tomato paste*

*½ teaspoon freshly ground pepper*

*5 teaspoons sea salt*

*2 tablespoons extra-virgin olive oil*

*¼ cup freshly grated Parmigiano-Reggiano*

Heat the remaining 2 tablespoons of olive oil in a large sauté pan over medium-high heat. Add the onion, celery, carrot, rosemary, sage, garlic, and bay leaf. Sauté until the vegetables are tender, about 10 minutes. Add the meat and diced tomato to the vegetable mixture and cook, stirring, until mixed, about 1 minute. Add the water, tomato paste, and pepper. Bring to a boil and cook on the stove 45 minutes. Or transfer to a clay pot, cover, reduce the oven to 300°F, and bake 45 minutes at a simmer. A thin layer of oil should remain on top of the sauce. Do not discard; it is full of flavor.

Bring 5 quarts of water and the 5 teaspoons of salt to a boil in a large stockpot. Add the pasta and cook 1 to 2 minutes. Taste the pasta before draining to ensure that it is cooked. Transfer to a colander to drain. Add the pasta to the pan with the ragù and toss to coat evenly. Drizzle with the extra-virgin olive oil and add the parmigiano; mix well.

# FRESH PASTA TUBES WITH PORCINI MUSHROOMS AND PARMESAN
## Garganelli ai Porcini e Parmigiano

*When I lived in Italy, my friends and I made an annual trip to hunt for mushrooms at a secluded spot on a mountain in Emilia-Romagna. One year we found a single porcini so large—it was the size of a melon—that it fed all five of us. I love the combination of porcini and fresh pasta tubes, such as garganelli from Emilia-Romagna. Garganelli are made by simultaneously wrapping each small piece of pasta dough around a smooth dowel and pressing it against a comb-like tool called a pettine. The pettine creates grooved impressions to help grab the sauce. (A smooth, round pencil and a clean, new comb can be used as substitutes for the dowel and pettine.)*

1 ounce dried porcini mushrooms

1 cup hot water

1 recipe Basic Pasta (page 21)

½ cup olive oil

2 shallots, chopped

2 garlic cloves, smashed and chopped

1 tablespoon chopped fresh Italian parsley

6 ounces fresh porcini or shiitake mushrooms, thinly sliced

½ cup dry white wine

5 teaspoons sea salt, plus extra for seasoning

Freshly ground pepper

2 tablespoons unsalted butter

¾ cup freshly grated Parmigiano-Reggiano

1 tablespoon extra-virgin olive oil

Place the porcini in a small bowl and cover with the hot water. Let sit 30 minutes. Remove the porcini from the water with your hands and transfer to a colander to drain. Strain the liquid to eliminate any sand and reserve. Squeeze the porcini to eliminate any excess liquid. Chop and set aside.

Prepare the pasta as directed on page 21. Let sit 30 minutes.

Roll out the pasta dough into two 48-inch sheets as described in steps 1 to 6 under "To roll out strands and ribbons" on page 22. Cut each sheet crosswise into four 12-inch lengths. Next, cut each sheet into 1½-inch squares. Roll the corner of each square around the dowel, or pencil, and then roll the pasta around the dowel while pressing firmly against the *pettine* or comb. Transfer to a flour-dusted platter. Let dry at least 2 hours.

Heat the olive oil in a large sauté pan over medium-high heat. Add the shallots, garlic, and parsley and cook until soft, about 5 minutes. Add the fresh porcini. Cook until the mushrooms become crispy, about 5 minutes. Add the dried porcini and wine; cook until the wine is evaporated, about 5 minutes. Add the reserved soaking liquid from the porcini. Cook the mixture until the liquid is reduced by half, 10 to 15 minutes. Add a pinch of the salt and pepper.

Bring 5 quarts of water and the 5 teaspoons of salt to a boil in a large stockpot over high heat. Add the garganelli and cook 2 to 3 minutes. Transfer to a colander to drain. Add to the pan with the mushrooms. Add the butter and toss until the butter is melted and well blended. Add the parmigiano and mix well. Drizzle the pasta with the extra-virgin olive oil.

# BUTTERNUT SQUASH PASTA FILLED WITH
## A BUTTERNUT SQUASH, PARMESAN, AND WALNUT FILLING
### Cappellacci alla Zucca

SERVES 6

The shape of this pasta inspired its name, which means "ugly hat." Cappellacci are the most popular stuffed pasta in Emilia-Romagna; the filling and sauce change from city to city. Deceptively simple, these "hats" are a wonderful way to enjoy an autumn harvest. They can be topped with just browned butter and sage, or with the addition of tomato sauce, which is how I prefer them.

One 4-pound
butternut squash

2 tablespoons sea salt,
plus extra for seasoning

1 ½ cups freshly grated
Parmigiano-Reggiano

¼ cup walnuts, toasted
and chopped

¼ teaspoon freshly
grated nutmeg

Freshly ground pepper

2 cups all-purpose flour,
plus extra for dredging

1 large egg, beaten

1 cup Salsa di Pomodoro
(page 24)

30 whole fresh sage
leaves, plus 1 tablespoon
chopped fresh sage

½ cup dry white wine

1 cup olive oil

2 tablespoons
unsalted butter

Preheat the oven to 350°F.

Cut the squash in half and remove the seeds. Place in a baking dish, cut-side up. Sprinkle with a generous amount of salt and bake until tender, about 2 hours. Scrape the meat out of the shell; if too watery, place in a small baking dish and bake until the liquid evaporates, about 20 minutes. Purée the squash until smooth in a food processor or with a potato masher.

Combine 1 ¼ cups of the squash purée, 1 cup of the parmigiano, the walnuts, nutmeg, and a pinch of salt and pepper in a medium bowl. Set aside.

Combine the flour and 1 teaspoon of the salt on a flat work surface or in a shallow bowl. Shape into a small mound. Make a well in the center and pour 1 ¼ cups of the remaining squash purée into the center. Mix and knead the dough as described in the Step-by-Step Guide for Making Pasta on page 21. Roll out the pasta as described in steps 1 and 2 under "To roll out Sheets" on page 22. Reserve any remaining squash purée for another use.

Brush each 24-inch sheet of pasta with some of the beaten egg. Cut into 4-inch squares with a fluted pastry cutter. Arrange a small mound of the filling (about 1 tablespoon) in the center of each square. Fold in half, corner to corner, to form a triangle. Gently place one finger on each edge to push out the air and seal the edges. (This also helps to prevent the stuffing from spilling out the sides.) Fold the uncut edge over and pull the corners around to the center to form the "hat" shape. Transfer the cappellacci to a flour-dusted platter and sprinkle with a light coating of flour to help dry the pasta.

Pour the tomato sauce into a large sauté pan and heat over medium heat.

Put some flour for dredging in a shallow bowl and set aside. Place the whole sage leaves in a small bowl. Cover with the wine and let sit 5 minutes. Heat the olive oil in a small sauté pan with high sides. Remove the sage leaves from the wine, one at a time, and coat lightly with the flour. Add to the pan and cook until crispy, about 2 minutes. Transfer to a paper towel–lined plate. Sprinkle lightly with salt. Melt the butter in a small sauté pan. Add the chopped sage and cook until the butter is browned, 1 to 2 minutes. Add a pinch of salt.

Bring 5 quarts of water and the remaining 5 teaspoons of salt to a boil in a large stockpot over high heat. Add the pasta and cook 2 to 3 minutes.

Spoon a small portion of tomato sauce onto each of 6 individual serving plates. Gently remove the pasta from the water with a slotted spoon and divide among the plates. Sprinkle with the remaining ½ cup of parmigiano. Tuck the fried sage among the cappellacci and pour the butter over the top at the table.

## *Rotolino di Pasta all'Emiliana*

---

SERVES 8

1 recipe Basic Pasta
(page 21)

¼ cup olive oil, plus extra
for drizzling

1 garlic clove, smashed

10 ounces shiitake
mushrooms, sliced

1 tablespoon chopped
fresh Italian parsley

3 cups ricotta

1 cup freshly grated
Parmigiano-Reggiano

3 ½ cups milk

5 teaspoons sea salt,
plus extra for seasoning

Freshly ground
black pepper

7 tablespoons
unsalted butter

½ cup all-purpose flour

¼ teaspoon freshly
grated nutmeg

Freshly ground
white pepper

1 pound thinly sliced
boiled ham

¾ pound thinly
sliced provolone

½ cup peeled, seeded, and
diced tomato (optional)

¼ cup whole fresh Italian
parsley leaves (optional)

*One year on my Chef's Tour we visited a friend near Modena. His grandmother had taken over the stove in the family restaurant to cook for us that day. She made this pasta, and the dough was perfect. The texture was like silk; the flavor brought forth the essence of flour and egg. Her many years of experience making fresh pasta were very apparent in every delicate bite.*

Prepare the pasta as directed on page 21. Let sit 30 minutes.

Preheat the oven to 400°F.

Heat 2 tablespoons of the olive oil in a large sauté pan over medium-high heat. Add the garlic and cook until it begins to brown, about 3 minutes. Remove the garlic and add the shiitakes and parsley. Sauté until the mushrooms are crispy, about 5 minutes. Combine the ricotta and ¾ cup of the parmigiano in a large bowl. Add the mushrooms and 1 cup of the milk. Add a pinch of salt and black pepper.

Slowly bring the remaining 2 ½ cups of milk to a low boil in a medium saucepan over medium-low heat. Melt 5 tablespoons of the butter in a large saucepan over medium heat. Add the flour to the butter and cook, stirring, until the flour is well incorporated, about 2 minutes. Whisk in the milk, nutmeg, and a pinch of salt and of white pepper. Cook until the mixture becomes thick, about 10 minutes. Remove from the heat. Drizzle a small amount of olive oil over the top of the béchamel sauce to prevent a skin from forming.

Roll out the pasta as described in steps 1 and 2 under "To roll out sheets" on page 22. Cut each 24-inch pasta sheet crosswise in half.

Bring 5 quarts of water, the 5 teaspoons of salt, and the remaining 2 tablespoons of olive oil

to a boil in a large stockpot over high heat. Add the pasta and cook until al dente, about 2 minutes. Transfer to a colander to drain.

Spread a small amount of oil on a flat work surface or large baking sheet. Lay the 4 pasta sheets on the olive oil so that the wider edges are at the top and the bottom. Divide the ricotta mixture among the pasta and spread over each sheet, leaving a 3-inch border on the top and a 1-inch border on the bottom and sides. Arrange an equal number of ham slices over each ricotta-topped pasta sheet. Top with the provolone. Gently roll each sheet into a cylinder, starting at the bottom and rolling towards the 3-inch border at the top.

Spread equal amounts of béchamel sauce into two 13-by-9-by-2-inch baking dishes. Trim the edges of each pasta roll back to where the filling starts. Cut each cylinder into 6 slices, about 1 inch thick. Arrange over the béchamel. Sprinkle the remaining ¼ cup of parmigiano over the top and dot with the remaining 2 tablespoons of butter. Bake 10 minutes. Set under the broiler to brown. Sprinkle with the tomato and parsley, if desired.

## DELICATE FRESH CRÊPES WITH A SPINACH-RICOTTA FILLING
### Crespelle alla Fiorentina

◉

SERVES 6

The French cooks once employed by Florence's nobility introduced crespelle to Italy. Like its cousin the French crêpe, the Italian version is prepared as a sweet or savory, and varies from one region to the next. This version, which incorporates a Florentine classic combination of spinach and cheese, is easy to make and can be prepared ahead of time. The béchamel sauce gives the impression of a rich, creamy dish, but the taste is light and fresh.

To make the crespelle: Beat the egg yolks, egg, and salt together in a medium bowl, using a whisk. Add the butter and mix well. Add the flour and stir until smooth. Gradually add the milk, whisking continuously.

Heat an 8-inch, nonstick sauté pan over medium-high heat. Wipe the inside of the pan with a small amount of oil. Pour in just enough batter, about 1/4 cup, to coat the bottom of the pan, swirling the pan to evenly distribute the batter. Cook until firm and evenly browned, about 1 minute. Turn and cook the other side about 1 minute. Transfer to a flat work surface to cool. Repeat until all of the batter is used. Once the crespelle are cool, stack between sheets of wax paper or directly on top of one another. Wrap loosely in a damp towel to prevent them from drying out.

To make the filling: Bring 2 quarts of water and the 2 teaspoons of salt to a boil in a medium stockpot over high heat. Add the spinach and cook until tender, about 5 minutes. Transfer to a colander to drain. Let cool. Squeeze the spinach between your hands to eliminate any excess liquid. Chop into a fine mixture.

Melt the butter in a large sauté pan over medium-high heat. Add the spinach, shallots, and garlic. Cook until the shallots are tender, about 5 minutes. Transfer to a medium bowl. Add the ricotta and parmigiano. Add a pinch of salt and pepper. Transfer to a pastry bag with a 1-inch tip.

To make the béchamel sauce: Slowly bring the milk to a low boil in a medium saucepan over medium-low heat. Melt the butter in a large saucepan over medium heat. Add the flour to the butter and cook, stirring, until the flour is well incorporated, about 2 minutes. Whisk in the milk, nutmeg, salt, and white pepper. Cook until the mixture becomes thick, about 10 minutes. Remove from the heat. Drizzle a small amount of olive oil over the top of the sauce to prevent a skin from forming.

Preheat the broiler. Stack the crespelle on top of each other, leaving a 2-inch border at the top of each one. Pipe out an equal amount of the filling onto the border of each crespelle and roll the crespelle firmly around the filling. Spoon half of the béchamel into a 13-by-9-by-2-inch baking dish. Arrange the crespelle in the baking dish. Spoon the remaining béchamel down the center of the crespelle. Cover the edges with foil to prevent burning, and place under the broiler. Cook until the béchamel begins to turn brown, 2 to 3 minutes. Spoon the tomato sauce over the top of the béchamel and garnish with the parsley.

For the crespelle:

2 large egg yolks

1 large egg

Pinch of sea salt

1 tablespoon unsalted butter, melted

1/2 cup all-purpose flour

1 cup plus 6 tablespoons milk

For the filling:

2 teaspoons sea salt, plus extra for seasoning

10 ounces baby spinach leaves

2 tablespoons unsalted butter

1/2 cup chopped shallots

1 garlic clove, chopped

2 cups ricotta

1/2 cup freshly grated Parmigiano-Reggiano

Freshly ground pepper

For the béchamel sauce:

4 cups milk

1/2 cup (1 stick) unsalted butter

1/2 cup all-purpose flour

1/2 teaspoon freshly grated nutmeg

1/2 teaspoon sea salt

1/2 teaspoon freshly ground white pepper

Olive oil for drizzling

1/2 cup Salsa di Pomodoro (page 24)

2 tablespoons chopped fresh Italian parsley

# CORKSCREW PASTA WITH A SAUCE OF ASSORTED OLIVES AND FRESH TOMATOES

*Fusilli al Sugo di Olive*

½ cup olive oil

1 cup diced onion

3 small dried peperoncini, broken into small pieces

1 teaspoon minced garlic

1 cup mixed green and black olives (at least 5 types, such as gaeta, colonna, kalamata, niçoise, picholine), pitted and cut into quarters if small, or into 6 wedges if large

10 fresh medium basil leaves, torn into small pieces

1 tablespoon chopped fresh Italian parsley

5 teaspoons sea salt, plus extra for seasoning

Freshly ground pepper

2 ripe medium tomatoes, peeled, seeded, and diced

2 cups Salsa di Pomodoro (page 24)

1 pound dry fusilli

1 cup freshly grated Parmigiano-Reggiano

2 tablespoons extra-virgin olive oil

SERVES 6

The olive harvest always follows the grape harvest in autumn. Some years when I arrive in Tuscany, I watch the vineyards being picked; other years I watch the olives being picked. One of Tuscany's most prolific crops, olives are either harvested and then pressed to make oil, or cured and enjoyed in robust dishes such as this one. If you aren't able to find an assortment of Tuscan olives, you can use an assortment of Greek, French, and Spanish olives.

Heat the olive oil in a large sauté pan over medium-high heat. Add the onion, peperoncini, and garlic. Cook until the onion is soft, about 5 minutes. Add the olives, basil, half of the parsley, and a pinch of salt and pepper. Add the tomatoes and mix well. Cook until the liquid evaporates, 2 to 3 minutes. Add the tomato sauce, bring to a boil, reduce the heat, and simmer 30 minutes.

Bring 5 quarts of water and the 5 teaspoons of salt to a boil in a large stockpot. Add the pasta and cook until al dente. Transfer to a colander to drain. Add to the pan with the olive sauce. Add the parmigiano, extra-virgin olive oil, and remaining parsley. Toss to mix well.

# FRESH HAND-TWISTED NOODLES
## TOPPED WITH A SAUSAGE SAUCE
### *Pici con Salsiccia*

SERVES 4

Fennel, a native vegetable of Tuscany, is found in many of the dishes of the area, from pasta to salads. It is so common that it grows wild by the side of the road. The seeds are used to flavor the fine sausages produced there, called finocchiona. I strongly recommend a fennel-flavored sausage for this recipe to provide the most authentic taste.

Prepare the pasta as directed on page 21. Let sit 30 minutes.

Roll out the pasta dough into two 48-inch sheets as described in steps 1 to 6 under "To roll out strands and ribbons" on page 22. Cut each sheet crosswise into 1/2-inch strips. On a clean work surface, hold one end of a strip while rolling the other with the palm of your other hand to form a twisted strand. Pull the ends gently to set the twist. Transfer to a flour-dusted platter. Continue in this fashion until all of the pasta has been twisted. Let dry at least 2 hours.

Heat the olive oil in a large sauté pan over medium-high heat. Add the sausage and cook until browned, 3 to 5 minutes. Add the shallots, garlic, and peperoncino. Cook until the shallots are tender, 3 to 5 minutes. Add the mushrooms, 1/2 teaspoon of the salt, and the pepper. Cook until the mushrooms begin to turn crispy, 5 to 10 minutes. Add the wine, bring to a boil, and cook until evaporated, about 5 minutes. Put the canned tomatoes in a medium bowl and break up with your hands. Add to the pan. Bring to a boil. Add the fresh tomatoes and half of the basil. Reduce the heat to low and simmer the sauce 45 to 50 minutes.

Bring 5 quarts of water and the remaining 5 teaspoons of salt to a boil in a large stockpot over high heat. Add the pasta and cook until al dente, about 2 to 3 minutes. Transfer to a colander to drain. Add to the pan with the sausage sauce and toss to coat evenly. Add the pecorino and remaining basil. Mix well.

1 recipe Basic Pasta (page 21)

2 tablespoons olive oil

3/4 pound mild Italian sausage with fennel, crumbled

2 shallots, minced

2 garlic cloves, chopped

1 small dried peperoncino, broken into small pieces

6 ounces fresh porcini, shiitake, or portobello mushrooms, thinly sliced

5 1/2 teaspoons sea salt

1/4 teaspoon freshly ground pepper

1/2 cup dry red wine

One 28-ounce can whole peeled tomatoes with their juice

4 ripe medium tomatoes, peeled, seeded, and diced

1/4 cup firmly packed fresh basil leaves, torn into small pieces

1/2 cup freshly grated Pecorino Romano

# WIDE PASTA RIBBONS IN A DUCK SAUCE
## *Pappardelle sull'Anatra*

SERVES 6

This dish reminds me of a trip to Tuscany for a Chef's Tour in the fall of 2000. We arrived at the Dievole Winery, producers of our Chianti Classico, in the middle of a rainstorm. We were all feeling as miserable as the weather. A feast had been prepared in our honor, so we sat down to eat despite our drooping spirits. All it took was a few bites of this pasta to change our mood, and it soon became quite a festive occasion.

Prepare the pasta as directed on page 21. Let sit 30 minutes.

Roll out the pasta dough into two 48-inch sheets as described in steps 1 to 6 under "To roll out strands and ribbons" on page 22. Cut each sheet crosswise into six 8-inch sheets. Stack on top of one another and cut into 3/4-inch-wide strips. Transfer to a flour-dusted platter. Let dry at least 2 hours.

Preheat the oven to 400°F.

Remove the neck and gizzards from the duck and set aside. Rinse the inside and outside of the duck with hot water. Trim the extra skin from around the neck and back. Cut in half lengthwise and remove the back. Discard. Cut each half into 4 pieces: Make a cut between the leg and breast, cut the breast in half, and cut the leg into 2 pieces below the thigh. Sprinkle with salt and pepper.

Heat 1 tablespoon of the olive oil in a large, ovenproof sauté pan over medium heat. Place the duck, skin-side down, in the pan. Cook slowly until crispy, about 20 minutes. Transfer the duck to a plate with a slotted spoon. Discard the oil from the pan, wipe clean, and return to the stove. Add the remaining 2 tablespoons of olive oil and heat over medium-high heat. Add the gizzards, onion, celery, carrot, sage, rosemary, and marjoram. Cook until the onion becomes soft, about 5 minutes. Add the duck, skin-side up, and cook 1 to 2 minutes. Add the wine and cook until reduced by a third. Add the tomatoes. Cover and bake in the oven until the meat falls from the bones, 45 minutes to 1 hour.

Remove the duck and gizzards from the pan. Let cool. Remove the meat from the bones. Discard the bones, skin, and any excess fat from the pan. Chop the meat and gizzards into a coarse mixture. Return to the sauté pan. Bring the liquid in the pan to a boil over medium-high heat.

Bring 5 quarts of water and the 5 teaspoons of salt to a boil in a large stockpot. Add the pasta and cook until al dente, about 2 minutes. Transfer to colander to drain, reserving some of the water. If the sauce seems too thick, add a little of the cooking water. Add the butter. Add the pasta, parmigiano, extra-virgin olive oil, and parsley. Toss to mix well. Transfer to a serving platter and sprinkle with freshly ground pepper.

1 recipe Basic Pasta (page 21)

One 5-pound fresh duck

5 teaspoons sea salt, plus extra for seasoning

Freshly ground pepper

3 tablespoons olive oil

3/4 cup finely diced onion

1/2 cup finely diced celery

1/2 cup finely diced carrot

1 tablespoon minced fresh sage

1 tablespoon minced fresh rosemary

1 tablespoon minced fresh marjoram

2 cups dry red wine

2 cups peeled, seeded, and diced tomatoes

1 tablespoon unsalted butter

3/4 cup freshly grated Parmigiano-Reggiano

2 tablespoons extra-virgin olive oil

2 tablespoons chopped fresh Italian parsley

# FRESH CRAB WITH TOMATOES AND THIN PASTA STRANDS
## *Spaghettini al Granchio*

**For the crab:**

1 teaspoon sea salt

1 large live crab
(about 3 pounds)

⅓ cup olive oil

2 garlic cloves, smashed

1 ½ teaspoons chopped
fresh Italian parsley

1 cup dry white wine

1 cup water

¼ cup olive oil

4 garlic cloves, smashed

1 small white onion, diced

1 dried peperoncino,
broken into small pieces

4 ripe medium tomatoes,
peeled, seeded, and diced

2 cups canned whole
peeled tomatoes with
their juice, puréed

¼ cup chopped fresh
Italian parsley

Freshly ground pepper

5 teaspoons sea salt

1 pound dry spaghettini

3 tablespoons
extra-virgin olive oil

A live crab should be used to make this recipe. The flavor of the entire dish depends on the juices that are released when the crab is cooked. You may be able to get the same effect by purchasing a crab that was just cooked, but if you buy only the meat, you'll rob yourself of the full taste of this pasta.

To prepare the crab: Bring 6 quarts of water and the salt to a boil over high heat. Add the crab and cook 2 to 3 minutes. Remove from the water. Remove the large body shell, reserving any liquid that escapes. Discard the shell. Cut the body, with legs, into quarters. Heat the olive oil in a large, high-sided sauté pan. Add the garlic. Cook until browned, about 1 minute, and remove. Add the crab and parsley and sauté 1 minute. Add the wine, cover, and cook 4 to 5 minutes. Transfer the crab to a bowl. Remove the meat from the remaining small shells, reserving any liquid that escapes. Set the meat aside. Return the small shells to the pan. Add the water and any reserved liquid. Bring to a boil over medium-high heat. Reduce to a third of its volume, about 3 minutes. Strain through a fine sieve set over a bowl, pressing firmly on the shells to extract all of the liquid. Set aside.

Heat the ¼ cup of olive oil in a large sauté pan over medium-high heat. Add the garlic and cook 1 minute. Add the onion and peperoncino. Cook until soft, about 3 minutes. Add the fresh tomatoes, puréed tomatoes, the reserved strained liquid, half of the parsley, and a pinch of pepper. Bring to a boil. Reduce the heat and cook at a simmer 30 minutes. Add the crabmeat.

Bring 5 quarts of water and the 5 teaspoons of salt to a boil in a large stockpot over high heat. Add the pasta and cook until al dente. Transfer to a colander to drain. Add to the pan with the crab sauce; toss to coat completely. Drizzle with the extra-virgin olive oil and top with the remaining parsley.

*Tagliatelle alle Fave*

3 garlic cloves

5 teaspoons sea salt,
plus extra for seasoning

4 pounds fresh
fava beans, shelled

⅓ cup plus 2 tablespoons
olive oil

1 small shallot, minced

6 fresh medium
basil leaves, torn into
small pieces

½ cup dry white wine

2 cups water

Freshly ground pepper

1 pound dry tagliatelle

⅓ cup extra-virgin
olive oil

1 ripe large tomato, peeled,
seeded, and diced

½ cup freshly grated
Pecorino Toscano or
Pecorino Romano

2 tablespoons shaved
ricotta salata (see head-
note on page 135)

*This pasta is so simple that it demands the best-tasting, freshest ingredients available. When fava beans are at their peak in spring, this dish is unequalled. Use the finest, most flavorful extra-virgin olive oil you can find. If it is from Umbria, all the better.*

Mince 1 garlic clove and smash the other 2. Set aside.

Bring 5 quarts of water and the 5 teaspoons of salt to a boil in a large stockpot over high heat. Add the fava beans and return to a boil. Remove immediately with a skimmer and leave the water in the pot. Remove the skins from the beans and discard. Place the beans in a small bowl and set aside.

Heat 2 tablespoons of the olive oil in a large sauté pan over medium-high heat. Add the shallot and smashed garlic. Cook until soft, about 1 minute. Add half of the basil and half of the fava beans and sauté 1 to 2 minutes. Add the wine and cook until evaporated completely, about 3 minutes. Add the water and bring to a boil. Cook until reduced by half, about 5 minutes. Transfer the mixture to the bowl of a food processor and purée.

Heat the remaining ⅓ cup of olive oil in a large sauté pan over medium-high heat. Add the minced garlic and the remaining basil. Cook 1 minute. Add the remaining cooked beans. Add a pinch of salt and pepper. Cook for 2 minutes. Add the puréed beans and mix well.

Return the water in the stockpot to a boil. Add the pasta and cook until al dente. Transfer to a colander to drain. Add to the pan with the fava bean sauce. Add the extra-virgin olive oil, tomato, and pecorino. Toss to mix well. Top with the ricotta salata.

# PASTA STRANDS WITH BLACK TRUFFLE SAUCE
## Spaghetti alla Norcina

SERVES 6

*Once while visiting the ancient town Perugia, in Umbria, my companion and I stopped at a small restaurant for lunch. On display was a black truffle that had been found by the owner. It was the size of a potato, and it perfumed the whole room. We were served this pasta dish, which was made with that special truffle. I was surprised by the exquisite balance of flavors brought on by the addition of the anchovies.*

Combine 2 of the truffles with ¼ cup of the olive oil in the container of a blender. Purée until a smooth consistency is reached.

Combine the remaining ¾ cup of olive oil, the anchovies, and garlic in a large sauté pan. Heat over medium heat. Add the wine and cook until nearly evaporated, 1 to 2 minutes.

Bring 5 quarts of water and the salt to a boil in a large stockpot over high heat. Add the pasta and cook until al dente. Transfer to a colander to drain, reserving ¼ cup of the cooking water. Add the pasta to the sauté pan with the anchovy mixture and toss to coat well. Add the truffle purée, parmigiano, parsley, and a pinch of pepper. If the sauce seems too thick, add some of the reserved water and toss to mix well. Shave the remaining truffle over the top of the pasta.

*3 medium black truffles (about 1 ounce each), or 3 canned truffles*

*1 cup extra-virgin olive oil*

*6 anchovy fillets, minced*

*3 garlic cloves, minced*

*¼ cup dry white wine*

*5 teaspoons sea salt*

*1 pound dry spaghetti*

*½ cup freshly grated Parmigiano-Reggiano*

*2 tablespoons chopped fresh Italian parsley*

*Freshly ground pepper*

# MUSSELS, ANCHOVIES, AND TOMATOES TOSSED WITH PASTA STRANDS
## *Spaghetti alle Cozze*

―◉―

SERVES 6

*When I was a teenager, on Sundays my family and I went to Punta Sabbioni, a beach near Venice famous for its mussels, which anyone could harvest. We'd bring a portable stove and cook the mussels right there on the shore. The taste of those mussels, straight from the sea, came flooding back to me the first time I ate this pasta in le Marche. Buy the freshest, best-tasting mussels you can find because they are the stars of this dish.*

To prepare the mussels: Heat the olive oil in a large, high-sided sauté pan over high heat. Add the mussels, garlic, parsley, and a pinch of pepper. Quickly squeeze the lemon over the mussels, then add it to the pan. Add the wine and cover. Cook until the mussels begin to open, 1 to 2 minutes. Be careful not to overcook. Spread the mussels on a baking sheet to cool. Remove the mussels from their shells by gently scraping with a small spoon. Discard the shells. Strain the liquid from the sauté pan into a medium saucepan and bring to a boil over medium-high heat. Cook until reduced by half, 2 to 3 minutes.

Heat the 1/3 cup of olive oil in a large sauté pan over medium-high heat. Add the anchovies, garlic, and peperoncino; cook 1 minute. Add the tomatoes and basil; cook 15 minutes. Add the reduced liquid from the mussels. Bring to a boil, reduce the heat, and simmer until the sauce becomes thick, 35 to 40 minutes.

Bring 5 quarts of water and the salt to a boil in a large stockpot over high heat. Add the pasta and cook until al dente. Transfer to a colander to drain. Add to the pan with the tomato sauce and toss to coat evenly. Add the mussels, extra-virgin olive oil, and parsley. Toss to mix well.

For the mussels:

1/4 cup olive oil

2 3/4 pounds mussels, well rinsed and debearded

4 garlic cloves, smashed

1 tablespoon chopped fresh parsley

Freshly ground pepper

1/2 lemon

1/2 cup dry white wine

1/3 cup olive oil

5 anchovy fillets, chopped

4 garlic cloves, smashed

1 dried peperoncino, broken into small pieces

One 28-ounce can plus 1 cup whole peeled tomatoes, with their juice, cut into thin strips

1/2 cup firmly packed fresh basil leaves, torn into small pieces

5 teaspoons sea salt

1 pound spaghetti

2 tablespoons extra-virgin olive oil

2 tablespoons chopped fresh Italian parsley

# HOLLOW, ROUND PASTA STRANDS
## IN A CLASSIC SAUCE OF PANCETTA AND EGGS
### *Bucatini alla Carbonara*

◎

SERVES 6

*Several years ago, I had the pleasure of eating this pasta in a small restaurant called La Cisterna, in the center of Rome. It was prepared in a traditional style using guanciale, or pork cheeks, and the waiter assembled it tableside. Today, most chefs prepare carbonara with pancetta and, to be sure that the eggs are cooked completely, the sauce is mixed in the pan. When you prepare this dish, be very careful not to scramble the eggs, or the sauce will be ruined.*

Heat the olive oil in a large sauté pan over medium-high heat. Add the pancetta and cook until browned and crispy, about 10 minutes.

Whisk together the whole eggs and egg yolks in a medium bowl. Add the pecorino, pepper, and 1/4 teaspoon of the salt. Set aside.

Bring 5 quarts of water and the remaining 5 teaspoons of salt to a boil in a large stockpot over high heat. Add the pasta and cook until al dente. Transfer to a colander to drain, reserving 2 to 3 tablespoons of the cooking water. Add the pasta to the pan with the pancetta. Add the egg mixture and toss to coat evenly. Cook the egg slightly. If the dish is too dry, add the reserved cooking water, 1 tablespoon at a time. Sprinkle with the parmigiano.

*1 tablespoon olive oil*

*10 ounces pancetta, diced*

*3 large eggs*

*3 large egg yolks*

*1 cup freshly grated pecorino*

*1 teaspoon freshly ground pepper*

*5 1/4 teaspoons sea salt*

*1 pound dry bucatini*

*1/4 cup freshly grated Parmigiano-Reggiano*

## Fusilli al Tonno

---

SERVES 6

¼ cup olive oil

¼ small onion,
finely diced

2 garlic cloves, minced

One 7-ounce can olive
oil–packed tuna, drained

½ cup assorted olives
(any cured Italian
varieties), pitted and
cut into thin wedges

3 tablespoons
chopped capers
(see Note on page 54)

¼ cup chopped fresh
Italian parsley

½ cup dry white wine

2 cups Salsa di Pomodoro
(page 24)

5 teaspoons sea salt,
plus extra for seasoning

Freshly ground pepper

1 pound dry fusilli

2 tablespoons
extra-virgin olive oil

Tuna imported from Italy is packed in olive oil, resulting in a flavor that is undeniably superior to any water-packed or vegetable oil–packed tuna. Italian tuna is widely available, and I suggest using it whenever possible. Look for packages that specify ventresca, which indicates that only the belly of the tuna—the most tender and moist part—is used.

Heat the olive oil in a medium saucepan over medium-high heat. Add the onion and garlic; cook until the garlic is browned, 2 to 3 minutes. Add the tuna and cook until all of the liquid evaporates, about 3 minutes. Add the olives, capers, and half of the parsley. Cook 1 minute. Add the wine and bring to a boil. Cook until evaporated entirely. Add the tomato sauce and bring to a boil. Cook 5 minutes and season with salt and pepper.

Bring 5 quarts of water and the 5 teaspoons of salt to a boil in a large stockpot over high heat. Add the pasta and cook until al dente. Transfer to a colander to drain. Add to the pan with the olive sauce. Add the extra-virgin olive oil and remaining parsley and toss to mix well.

# PASTA STRANDS WITH GARLIC, OLIVE OIL, AND DRIED RED PEPPER
## Spaghetti Aglio, Olio e Peperoncino

◉

SERVES 6

*This pasta dish is common everywhere in Italy, although it originated in Lazio. When I was still a teenager, my friends and I would gather at one of our parents' homes after an evening out and make this dish. We called it* Spaghetti a Mezzanotte, *"midnight spaghetti," because it could be prepared quickly and quietly late at night.*

5 ½ teaspoons sea salt

1 pound dry spaghetti

⅓ cup olive oil

5 garlic cloves, minced

2 dried peperoncini, broken into small pieces

2 tablespoons chopped fresh Italian parsley

½ cup freshly grated Parmigiano-Reggiano

3 tablespoons extra-virgin olive oil

Freshly ground pepper

Bring 5 quarts of water and 5 teaspoons of the salt to a boil in a large stockpot over high heat. Add the pasta and cook until al dente.

While the pasta is cooking, combine the olive oil with the garlic and peperoncini in a large sauté pan. Cook over medium-high heat until the garlic begins to brown, about 3 minutes. Add the parsley and the remaining ½ teaspoon of salt.

Transfer the pasta to a colander to drain, reserving ¼ cup of the cooking water. Add the pasta to the pan with the olive oil–garlic mixture. Add the parmigiano, extra-virgin olive oil, and a pinch of pepper. Toss to mix well. If it seems dry, add a little of the reserved cooking water.

# A Fiery Tomato Sauce with Small Pasta Tubes
## Penne all'Arrabbiata

Arrabbiata *means "angry," and this fiery dish is so named because it is said that one becomes red in the face when eating it. The heat comes from the peperoncino, a small red chile pepper used in great quantities in the southern regions. There was a time when the area was widely impoverished and food was so scarce that much of the flavor in southern Italians' basic diet came from peperoncini.*

Heat the olive oil in a medium saucepan over medium-high heat. Add the garlic and cook until browned, about 3 minutes. Add the peperoncini and basil. Cook 1 minute. Add the tomato sauce. Bring to a boil, reduce the heat, and simmer 5 to 10 minutes.

Bring 5 quarts of water and 5 teaspoons of the salt to a boil in a large stockpot over high heat. Add the pasta and cook until al dente. Transfer to a colander to drain. Add to the pan with the tomato sauce. Add the extra-virgin olive oil, remaining 1/2 teaspoon of salt, and the pepper. Toss to mix well.

3 tablespoons olive oil

4 garlic cloves, sliced

1 1/2 dried peperoncini, broken into small pieces

6 fresh medium basil leaves, torn into small pieces

2 cups Salsa di Pomodoro (page 24)

5 1/2 teaspoons sea salt

1 pound dry penne

3 tablespoons extra-virgin olive oil

1/4 teaspoon freshly ground pepper

◉

SERVES 6

1 tablespoon olive oil

6 ounces pancetta, julienned

1 small white onion, diced

1 dried peperoncino, broken into small pieces

2 ripe large tomatoes, peeled, seeded, and diced

2 cups canned whole peeled tomatoes with their juice, puréed

6 fresh medium basil leaves, torn into small pieces

2 tablespoons sea salt

¼ teaspoon freshly ground pepper

1 pound dry perciatelli

½ cup freshly grated Pecorino Romano

3 tablespoons extra-virgin olive oil

Pancetta is salt-cured pork seasoned with pepper and spices. It is favored by Romans and included in many of their most famous pasta dishes. Do not confuse pancetta with bacon, which is smoked; they taste entirely different. Ask for pancetta at the deli counter or meat department where you shop. It is also found in many delicatessens.

Heat the olive oil in a large sauté pan over medium-high heat. Add the pancetta and cook until it becomes crispy, about 10 minutes. Add the onion and peperoncino and cook until the onion becomes soft, 3 to 5 minutes. Add the fresh tomatoes, puréed tomatoes, basil, 1 teaspoon of the salt, and the pepper. Bring to a boil. Reduce the heat and simmer 30 minutes.

Bring 5 quarts of water and the remaining 5 teaspoons of salt to a boil in a large stockpot over high heat. Add the pasta and cook until al dente. Transfer to a colander to drain. Add to the pan with the tomato sauce. Add the pecorino and extra-virgin olive oil. Toss to mix well.

### *Cavatappi Tonno e Carciofi*

---

Italian artichoke varieties number in the hundreds, and in the spring the markets are full of artichokes of all sizes and shades of green. Some have long stems still full of leaves. Artichokes are so loved by Italians that they are eaten raw or cooked, added to pasta sauces, or fried as an appetizer. This recipe is one of my favorite ways to enjoy them. Select artichokes with long stems to enjoy their full potential.

3 medium artichokes (about 1 pound total)

Juice of ½ lemon

⅓ cup olive oil

½ medium sweet onion, diced

3 garlic cloves, smashed

1 small dried peperoncino, broken into small pieces

2 tablespoons chopped fresh Italian parsley

5 teaspoons sea salt, plus extra for seasoning

Freshly ground pepper

½ cup dry white wine

2 cups Salsa di Pomodoro (page 24)

One 7-ounce can olive oil–packed tuna, drained

8 small Yukon gold potatoes, peeled and cut into ¼-inch-thick slices

1 pound dry cavatappi

2 tablespoons extra-virgin olive oil

Trim all but 1¼ inches away from the artichoke stems. Remove the tough, dark green outer leaves. Trim the top of each artichoke, leaving 1¼ inches above the base, and cut the artichoke in half, lengthwise. Remove the center, called the choke, and discard. Cut the artichokes into a julienne and put in a medium bowl. Cover with cold water and add the lemon juice to prevent discoloration. Set aside.

Heat the olive oil in a large sauté pan over medium-high heat. Transfer the artichokes to a colander to drain and add to the pan. Add the onion, garlic, and peperoncino and cook until the artichokes begin to brown on the edges, about 5 minutes. Add half of the parsley. Add a pinch of the salt and pepper. Add the wine and cook until evaporated, about 5 minutes. Add the tomato sauce and tuna. Bring to a boil over medium-high heat and cook for 5 to 7 minutes. Season with salt and pepper.

Bring 5 quarts of water and the 5 teaspoons of salt to a boil in a large stockpot over high heat. Add the potatoes and pasta and cook until the pasta is al dente. Transfer to a colander to drain. Add the potatoes and pasta to the sauté pan with the artichoke sauce and toss to coat evenly. Add the extra-virgin olive oil and remaining parsley and mix well.

# THIN PASTA STRANDS WITH SHRIMP AND SQUASH BLOSSOMS

## Vermicelli con Gamberi ai Fiori di Zucchine

SERVES 6

In spring and early summer when zucchine, which literally means "small squash," first appear, they are most tender and delicious, and the blossoms are at their peak. These zucchini flowers are prepared in many ways—from appetizers to desserts—and impart a seasonal quality to a dish. Any time I have the opportunity to eat these fiori, I take it.

Heat ¼ cup of the olive oil in a large sauté pan over medium-high heat. Add the shrimp, 2 of the garlic cloves, and half of the parsley. Cook until the shrimp begins to turn bright orange, about 1 minute. Add the wine and saffron. Bring to a boil. Cook until reduced by half, about 3 minutes.

Heat the remaining 2 tablespoons of olive oil in a separate sauté pan over high heat. Add the remaining garlic clove and cook 1 minute. Add the zucchini and cook until crispy on both sides, about 3 minutes per side, stirring frequently. Add the zucchini blossoms and cook 1 minute. Add the zucchini, blossoms, and garlic to the shrimp. Add a pinch of salt and pepper.

Bring 5 quarts of water and the 5 teaspoons of salt to a boil in a large stockpot over high heat. Add the pasta and cook until al dente. Transfer to a colander to drain, reserving 1 tablespoon of the cooking water. Add the pasta to the pan with the zucchini mixture. Add the butter and remaining parsley. Toss to mix well. Add the extra-virgin olive oil and mix well. If the pasta is dry, add the reserved cooking water.

¼ cup plus 2 tablespoons olive oil

¾ pound large shrimp, peeled and deveined

3 garlic cloves, minced

1 tablespoon chopped fresh Italian parsley

1 cup dry white wine

½ teaspoon saffron threads

8 small zucchini (about 4 inches long), cut on the diagonal into ⅓-inch-thick slices

8 zucchini blossoms, stemmed and cut into ¼-inch strips

5 teaspoons sea salt, plus extra for seasoning

Freshly ground pepper

1 pound dry vermicelli

1 tablespoon unsalted butter

2 tablespoons extra-virgin olive oil

## Conchiglie con Rucola alla Molisana

◎

SERVES 6

¼ cup olive oil

2 garlic cloves, chopped

½ small onion, diced

1 cup loosely packed
fresh basil leaves, torn
into small pieces

2 ripe medium tomatoes,
peeled, seeded, and diced

2 bunches baby arugula,
cut into 1-inch pieces

2 cups Salsa di Pomodoro
(page 24)

5 teaspoons sea salt,
plus extra for seasoning

Freshly ground pepper

1 pound dry conchiglie

½ cup freshly grated
Parmigiano-Reggiano

¼ cup extra-virgin
olive oil

Unlike many greens that rely on other ingredients for flavor enhancement, arugula is robust and strongly flavored on its own. It has a slightly peppery taste, especially the arugula grown in Abruzzo and Molise. In this pasta recipe the arugula, basil, and tomato are a great combination, which tastes like a summer garden. It is one of our customers' favorites at Il Fornaio, and they are always pleased to see it on the menu.

Heat the olive oil in a large sauté pan over medium-high heat. Add the garlic and onion and cook until the garlic begins to brown, 2 to 3 minutes. Add the basil and fresh tomato and cook 3 to 5 minutes. Add the arugula and tomato sauce. Season with salt and pepper.

Bring 5 quarts of water and the 5 teaspoons of salt to a boil in a large stockpot over high heat. Add the pasta and cook until al dente. Transfer to a colander to drain. Add to the pan with the tomato sauce. Add the parmigiano and extra-virgin olive oil. Toss to mix well.

## Pasta Strands with a Lamb Sauce
*Chitarrine al Sugo d'Agnello*

SERVES 6

*Chitarrine, or "guitar string," pasta is shaped by placing a sheet of pasta on a chitarra, a square frame lined with thin metal strings, which resembles a guitar. A rolling pin is rolled over the pasta, pushing it against the strings, which cuts through the dough to form strands of pasta. You can cut the pasta with a knife if you don't have a chitarra.*

Prepare the pasta as directed on page 21. Let sit 30 minutes.

Roll out the pasta dough into two 48-inch sheets as described in steps 1 to 6 under "To roll out strands and ribbons" on page 22. Cut each sheet crosswise into four 12-inch lengths.

Cut the noodles with a *chitarra* if you have one, or with the pasta maker attachment, cut each 12-inch sheet into small flat noodles 1/16 inch wide. Hang to dry for at least 2 hours.

Heat 2 tablespoons of the olive oil in a large sauté pan over medium-high heat. Add the lamb and cook over high heat until browned, about 3 minutes. Add the onion, carrots, celery, garlic, peperoncino, thyme, marjoram, and bay leaf.

Cook until the vegetables are soft, about 5 minutes. Add the wine and cook until completely evaporated, about 5 minutes. Place the tomatoes in a medium bowl and break into small pieces using your hands. Add to the pan. Bring to a boil, reduce the heat, and simmer 30 minutes. Season with salt and pepper.

Heat the remaining 1 tablespoon of olive oil in a medium sauté pan over medium heat. Add the bell pepper and cook until soft, about 3 minutes.

Bring 5 quarts of water and the 5 teaspoons of salt to a boil in a large stockpot over high heat. Add the pasta and cook 2 to 3 minutes. Transfer to a colander to drain. Add to the pan with the lamb sauce. Transfer the bell pepper to the pasta with a slotted spoon. Add the pecorino and extra-virgin olive oil. Toss to mix well.

---

1 recipe Basic Pasta (page 21)

3 tablespoons olive oil

10 ounces lean lamb stew meat, cut into 1/2-inch cubes

1/2 cup finely diced white onion

1/3 cup finely diced carrots

1/3 cup finely diced celery

3 garlic cloves, minced

1 dried peperoncino, broken into small pieces

1 tablespoon chopped fresh thyme

1 tablespoon chopped fresh marjoram

1 fresh bay leaf

1 cup dry red wine

One 28-ounce can whole peeled tomatoes with their juice

5 teaspoons sea salt, plus extra for seasoning

Freshly ground pepper

1/2 cup finely diced red bell pepper

5 tablespoons freshly grated Pecorino Romano

2 tablespoons extra-virgin olive oil

ALONG THE SOUTHERN SHORELINE

"The land of sea and sunshine" is how many describe the regions that comprise the southern end of Italy's mainland. A warm climate, fertile soil, and a prosperous shoreline heavily influence the foods from the four regions located in the heel of the boot—Campania, Basilicata, Calabria, Puglia.

For centuries, the Mediterranean environment of these regions has been an invitation to other civilizations to travel across Italy's heel. Many left such a strong imprint that the history of Italian cuisine was altered forever. It is believed that South American explorers planted the first tomato seeds in these southern parts. Other vegetables are also grown here in abundance. The fiery peperoncino is as common as the tomato. Cauliflower, zucchini, and rapini (a relative of turnips and cabbage that looks like broccoli, also called broccoli rabe) are prominent ingredients in many of the area's most popular pasta dishes.

Three seas—Adriatico, Mar Tirreno, and Mar Ionico—meet at the southernmost part of Italy's mainland, providing an abundance of seafood. The different currents and temperatures of the seas influence the types of shellfish and fish that populate the waters in these regions. Shellfish such as clams, mussels, and scallops are especially popular in pasta. The majority are available straight from the boat early in the morning in most towns.

Sheep's and cow's milk cheeses, such as pecorino and ricotta, are equally loved and used in the cookery of these regions. It is the water buffalo of Campania, however, that get all the glory, thanks to the creamy, pure taste of the fresh mozzarella they produce.

Fresh meat is enjoyed in small portions, but it is overshadowed by the popularity of sausages. This area is celebrated for the outstanding pork sausages that are so deliciously presented in many pasta sauces. Lamb, too, is favored and frequently added to pasta.

Perhaps the most famous crop of the southern regions is durum wheat, from which semolina flour is made. Semolina and water are two ingredients that have had more influence on Italian cuisine than any other combination of foods. This culinary marvel is the cornerstone of the dry pastas that have originated in these regions, from the beloved spaghetti noodle to the universal maccheroni, from Puglia's well-loved orecchiette to the familiar penne.

I cannot imagine a world without humble dry pasta and have honored it with the classic recipes that have emerged from the regions featured in this chapter.

## CAMPANIA

*Linguine Mare Chiaro al Cartoccio* 124
PASTA RIBBONS, MUSSELS, CLAMS,
SHRIMP, SCALLOPS, AND TOMATO
SAUCE COOKED IN PARCHMENT

*Strangolaprieti alla Sorrentina* 126
POTATO DUMPLINGS IN A
TOMATO SAUCE WITH FRESH BASIL
AND MELTED MOZZARELLA

*Spaghettini al Filetto di Pomodoro* 127
A CLASSIC COMBINATION OF
THIN PASTA STRANDS AND
TOMATO-BASIL SAUCE

*Vermicelli alle Vongole* 129
THIN PASTA STRANDS WITH
FRESH CLAMS AND
GARLIC–WHITE WINE SAUCE

*Tagliolini al Limone* 131
PRAWNS AND PASTA RIBBONS
WITH PARSLEY PESTO

*Pasta al Forno* 134
PASTA TUBES BAKED WITH CHEESE,
EGGPLANT, AND TOMATO SAUCE

## BASILICATA

*Pennette con Ricotta Salata* 135
SMALL PASTA TUBES AND
LAMB SAUCE WITH AGED RICOTTA

*Spaghetti alla Lucana* 137
ROASTED PEPPERS AND CLAMS
WITH PASTA STRANDS

## CALABRIA

*Rigatoni alla Calabrese* 138
FAT PASTA TUBES WITH
ITALIAN SAUSAGE AND TOMATOES

## PUGLIA

*Cavatelli con Braciolette* 139
SMALL PASTA SHELLS TOPPED
WITH A CLASSIC MEAT ROLL

*Fazzoletti con Cozze e Fagioli* 140
FRESH PASTA "HANDKERCHIEFS" WITH
MUSSELS, BEANS, AND TOMATOES

*Orecchiette con Cime di Rapa* 143
"LITTLE EARS" OF PASTA WITH
RAPINI, ANCHOVIES, AND GARLIC

## Linguine Mare Chiaro al Cartoccio

◎

½ cup plus ⅓ cup olive oil

4 garlic cloves, smashed

18 small, fresh clams,
well rinsed
(see Note on page 72)

18 mussels, well rinsed
and debearded

3 cups canned whole
peeled tomatoes, cut
lengthwise into strips

6 fresh medium
basil leaves, torn into
small pieces

18 large shrimp, peeled
and deveined

18 large scallops

¼ cup chopped fresh
Italian parsley

2 tablespoons sea salt

¼ teaspoon freshly
ground pepper

1 cup dry white wine

1 pound dry linguine

2 tablespoons
extra-virgin olive oil

1 egg, beaten

Enclosed in a parchment paper wrapping, this favorite dish of Campania makes for a stunning presentation when "unwrapped" at the table. Not only do you release the aromas, you also unveil an incredible selection of shellfish, which are so abundant in the region. After the paper is sealed and inflated, you can paint a design, such as a fish or flower, on the paper with the egg. It isn't absolutely necessary to bake the pasta in parchment. If you choose not to, cook the spaghetti one minute longer and serve it topped with the shellfish.

Heat ¼ cup of the olive oil in a large sauté pan over medium-high heat. Add 3 of the garlic cloves and cook 2 to 3 minutes. Add the clams and mussels in their shells. Cover and cook until the shells open, 2 to 3 minutes. Transfer to a bowl. Strain the liquid and reserve in a separate bowl.

Wipe out the pan and return to the stove. Add ⅓ cup of the olive oil and heat over high heat. Add the remaining garlic clove. Cook 1 minute. Add the tomatoes and basil and cook 3 to 5 minutes. Add the reserved liquid from the clams and mussels. Bring the mixture to a boil. Reduce the heat and simmer 25 minutes.

Meanwhile, heat the remaining ¼ cup of olive oil in a large sauté pan over medium-high heat. Add the shrimp, scallops, half of the parsley, 1 teaspoon of the salt, and the pepper. Cook 1 to 2 minutes. Add the wine and cook 1 minute. Remove the shrimp and scallops. Cook until the wine is reduced by half, about 2 minutes.

Preheat the oven to 500°F.

Cut a piece of parchment paper twice as wide as a large ovenproof platter. Arrange it on the platter so that only half is covering the platter and the other half is hanging over the side.

Bring 5 quarts of water and the remaining 5 teaspoons of salt to a boil in a large stockpot over high heat. Add the pasta and cook until al dente. Transfer to a colander to drain.

Add the clams, mussels, shrimp, and scallops to the tomato sauce, reserving about 6 of each for a garnish. Add the pasta to the tomato sauce and toss to coat well. Transfer to the parchment paper–covered platter. Arrange the reserved seafood around the edges of the pasta. Drizzle with the extra-virgin olive oil and sprinkle with the remaining parsley. Brush the edges of the parchment with the egg. Fold the empty half of the parchment over the top of the pasta and press the edges together to seal. Roll each edge into a tight coil, but before sealing completely, blow into the pouch to fill it with air. Finish sealing and brush the top with a light coat of egg in a decorative design.

Bake until browned, 5 to 10 minutes (it may take longer to brown in an oven with the broiler on the bottom), being careful to keep it away from the heating element to prevent the paper from catching on fire. Turn after 2 to 3 minutes to bake evenly. For a dramatic presentation, place on the table and gently tear the parchment open with a spoon and fork, starting in the center.

# POTATO DUMPLINGS IN A TOMATO SAUCE
## WITH FRESH BASIL AND MELTED MOZZARELLA
### Strangolaprieti alla Sorrentina

---

SERVES 6

The legend behind this dish is that priests were so infatuated with gnocchi that they ate them in great quantities, and one priest in particular ate so many that he "strangled," or suffocated himself. In this recipe Campania's buffalo mozzarella is added, making it all the more appealing. There is no substitute for the creamy, lush taste of fresh mozzarella; avoid the packaged, rubbery kind.

1 recipe Basic Gnocchi
(page 23)

2 cups Salsa di Pomodoro
(page 24)

5 teaspoons sea salt

8 ounces fresh
mozzarella, diced

6 fresh medium
basil leaves, torn into
small pieces

Prepare the gnocchi dough as directed. Roll it into a 5-inch-long cylinder and then 5 longer cylinders, as directed in the Step-by-Step Guide for Shaping Dumplings on page 23. Cut into ³/4-inch pieces. Press each piece against the tines on the back of a fork while gently rolling it down. Transfer to a flour-dusted plate with a spatula.

Pour the tomato sauce into a large sauté pan and bring to a boil. Cook 1 minute. Reduce the heat to low and keep warm while the pasta is cooking.

Bring 5 quarts of water and the 5 teaspoons of salt to a boil in a large stockpot over high heat. Add the gnocchi and cook until they rise to the top, about 5 minutes. Transfer to a colander to drain. Add the mozzarella to the sauté pan with the tomato sauce. Cook 1 minute. Add the pasta and toss to mix well. Add the basil and mix well.

# A Classic Combination of Thin Pasta Strands and Tomato-Basil Sauce

*Spaghettini al Filetto di Pomodoro*

SERVES 6

Tomatoes, olive oil, and basil are the foundation for most Italian tomato sauces. Other ingredients are then added to distinguish the sauce regionally. This sauce is distinctive because those three primary ingredients are the stars of the dish. So use the most flavorful extra-virgin olive oil and vine-ripened tomatoes you can find.

Heat the olive oil in a large sauté pan over medium-high heat. Add the tomato, basil, 1/2 teaspoon of the salt, and the pepper. Cook 3 to 4 minutes. Add the tomato sauce and cook 5 minutes.

Bring 5 quarts of water and the remaining 5 teaspoons of salt to a boil in a large stockpot over high heat. Add the pasta and cook until al dente. Transfer to a colander to drain. Add to the pan with the tomato sauce. Add the extra-virgin olive oil and toss to mix well.

3 tablespoons olive oil

1 cup peeled, seeded, and diced ripe tomato

6 fresh medium basil leaves, torn into small pieces

5 1/2 teaspoons sea salt

1/4 teaspoon freshly ground pepper

2 cups Salsa di Pomodoro (page 24)

1 pound dry spaghettini

1/3 cup extra-virgin olive oil

# THIN PASTA STRANDS WITH FRESH CLAMS AND GARLIC–WHITE WINE SAUCE

## *Vermicelli alle Vongole*

SERVES 6

The very flavorful, abundant clam called veraci, found in the waters surrounding Naples, inspired this recipe. Pasta strands with clams seem to be a classic dish wherever clams are to be found—there is something about the way clams nest in the pasta and the open shells hold the sauce. In Naples, only veraci are used because they have an intense flavor of the sea and are less chewy than other clams. You may not be able to find veraci clams, so use fresh, local clams as a substitute.

**For the clams:**

3 tablespoons olive oil

3 pounds small, fresh clams, well rinsed (see Note on page 72)

4 garlic cloves, chopped

1 tablespoon chopped fresh parsley

½ lemon

½ cup dry white wine

5 teaspoons sea salt

¼ cup olive oil

2 garlic cloves, minced

1 dried peperoncino, torn into small pieces

2 tablespoons chopped fresh Italian parsley

½ cup dry white wine

1 pound dry vermicelli

2 tablespoons extra-virgin olive oil

Freshly ground pepper

To prepare the clams: Heat the olive oil in a large, high-sided sauté pan over high heat. Add the clams, garlic, and parsley. Quickly squeeze the lemon over the clams, then add it to the pan. Add the wine. Cover and bring to a boil. Cook until the clams begin to open, 1 to 2 minutes. Be careful not to overcook. Spread the clams on a baking sheet to cool. Strain the liquid into a medium bowl and reserve. Remove the clams from their shells by gently scraping with a small spoon. Reserve a few whole clams for garnish and reserve the empty shells.

Put the shells in a large stockpot. Add 5 quarts of water and the 5 teaspoons of salt; bring to a boil over high heat. Reduce the heat and simmer 30 minutes.

Heat the ¼ cup of olive oil in a large sauté pan over medium-high heat. Add the garlic, peperoncino, and half of the parsley. Cook until the garlic begins to brown, 1 to 2 minutes. Add the wine and cook until nearly evaporated, about 5 minutes. Add the clams and the reserved strained liquid. Bring to a boil. Reduce the heat to low and keep warm while the pasta is cooking.

Remove the shells from the water in the stockpot with tongs or a skimmer. Add enough water so that you have 5 quarts again. Bring to a boil over high heat. Add the pasta and cook until al dente. Transfer to a colander to drain. Add the pasta to the pan with the clams. Add the remaining parsley and toss to mix well. Drizzle with the extra-virgin olive oil and sprinkle with the pepper.

## A Good Soldier

When I was nineteen years old, I entered the military and was assigned to the job of cooking for the enlisted men. One day the officers' cook was ill and I was sent as a substitute. I prepared fresh pasta, and the officers loved it so much that I was asked back many times and eventually was promoted to officers' cook. We were stationed on Sant'Andrea, an island near Venice where the local residents ate mostly seafood. Soon I developed a friendship with a neighborhood fisherman, who pulled his boat up to the back of my kitchen to trade his seafood, including lots of clams, for our military frozen chickens. Midway through my duty I was joined by a chef from Naples. He taught me, when making *Vermicelli alle Vongole*, to boil empty clam shells in water before cooking the pasta for added flavor. I still think of him whenever I cook pasta with clams.

# PRAWNS AND PASTA RIBBONS WITH PARSLEY PESTO
## Tagliolini al Limone

SERVES 6

When I was in grammar school, my older sister, Marisa, followed me everywhere and always wanted to know what I was doing. One day I complained to my mother and she said, "Your sister is like the parsley, she wants to be in everything." Italian parsley is so easy to grow and so well loved that it appears in many dishes.

In this pasta dish parsley is used to make a robust sauce. On my Chef's Tour in 2000, we went to Sorrento for a colleague's wedding and joined friends at a restaurant called L'Antica Trattoria the night before the ceremony. While I'd had this pasta before, I'd never seen it presented so creatively. You can achieve the same striking presentation at home.

1 recipe Basic Pasta (page 21)

2 cups loosely packed fresh Italian parsley leaves

1/3 cup plus 3 tablespoons olive oil

1 tablespoon water

5 3/4 teaspoons sea salt

1/2 teaspoon freshly ground pepper

1/2 pound medium shrimp, peeled and deveined, cut in half

1/4 cup lemon-flavored vodka

1/2 cup fresh lemon juice

3 cups heavy whipping cream

1/2 teaspoon grated lemon zest

3 extra-large lemons, cut in half lengthwise and hollowed out

3 teaspoons caviar (about 1 ounce)

Prepare the pasta as directed on page 21. Let sit 30 minutes.

Roll out the pasta dough into two 48-inch sheets as described in steps 1 to 6 under "To roll out strands and ribbons" on page 22. Cut each sheet crosswise into four 12-inch lengths.

Using the pasta maker attachment, cut each sheet into flat ribbons 1/16 inch wide. Transfer to a flour-dusted platter and sprinkle with additional flour. Let dry at least 2 hours, moving the pasta around occasionally to prevent sticking.

Put the parsley in the bowl of a food processor and chop until fine. Gradually add 1/3 cup of the olive oil with the motor running. Add the water and process until completely blended. Add 1/2 teaspoon of the salt and 1/4 teaspoon of the pepper and pulse until combined with the parsley mixture. Set aside.

Heat the remaining 3 tablespoons of olive oil in a large sauté pan over medium-high heat. Add the shrimp and cook until they begin to turn bright orange, about 2 minutes. Add the vodka, 1/4 teaspoon of the salt, and the remaining 1/4 teaspoon pepper; cook until the vodka evaporates. Add the lemon juice and bring to a boil. Add the cream and lemon zest. Return to a boil, reduce the heat, and cook until the sauce becomes thick, about 5 minutes.

(continued on next page)

Bring 5 quarts of water and the remaining 5 teaspoons of salt to a boil in a large stockpot over high heat. Add the pasta and cook until al dente, 30 seconds to 3 minutes, depending on how dry the pasta is; taste to test. Transfer to a colander to drain. Add the pasta to the pan with the lemon-shrimp sauce. Place a spoonful of the parsley pesto on a plate. Cut a thin slice off the bottom of each hollowed-out lemon half so that it will sit flat. Arrange 1 lemon half on each plate over the pesto and arrange a portion of the pasta in the lemon. Top with 1/2 teaspoon of caviar.

## Sweet and Tart Citrus Flavor

The lemons in southern Italy are larger and sweeter than any I've tried elsewhere. Driving along the coast, you can see them everywhere. Many products are made with these incredible lemons including Limoncello, a lemon-flavored liqueur. It tastes sweet and tart at the same time, a little like sweetened lemon vodka, only better—and a great way to cleanse your palate at the end of a meal. While I've tried to make limoncello here in the United States, without the lemons of southern Italy, it's just not the same. Look for it here at a good liquor store or Italian deli, and try to buy one made in Sorrento; it's the best.

---

SERVES 6

*1 large round eggplant (about ¾ pound), cut into ¾-inch cubes*

*2 tablespoons plus 2 teaspoons sea salt*

*2 cups Salsa di Pomodoro (page 24)*

*Flour for dredging*

*1 ½ cups vegetable oil*

*1 pound dry pennette*

*3 fresh medium basil leaves, torn into small pieces*

*½ cup freshly grated Pecorino Romano*

*5 ounces fresh mozzarella, cut into ½-inch cubes*

*¼ pound sliced caciocavallo or provolone*

*2 tablespoons extra-virgin olive oil*

*1 tablespoon fresh bread crumbs*

A Campania specialty, caciocavallo is a cow's milk cheese that is aged to gain firmness, so it can be sliced or grated. The mild cheese is shaped into balls and hung on string. Its name roughly translates as "cheese of a horse," because it looks as though it could be slung over a horse like saddlebags.

Preheat the oven to 400°F.

Arrange the eggplant in a single layer on a paper towel–lined plate. Sprinkle 1 tablespoon of the salt over the eggplant and let sit for at least 1 hour to eliminate any excess moisture.

Pour the tomato sauce into a large sauté pan and bring to a boil over medium-high heat. Cook 1 minute. Reduce the heat to low and keep warm while the pasta is cooking.

Pat the eggplant dry with a paper towel. Place the flour in a shallow bowl and dredge the eggplant in the flour to coat evenly on all sides. Heat the vegetable oil in a large sauté pan over medium-high heat. Shake off any excess flour from the eggplant and add to the pan. Cook until browned and crispy, about 5 minutes. Transfer to a paper towel–lined plate to absorb any excess oil. Set aside.

Bring 5 quarts of water and the remaining 5 teaspoons of salt to a boil in a large stockpot over high heat. Add the pasta and cook until al dente. Transfer to a colander to drain. Add to the pan with the tomato sauce. Add the basil and ¼ cup of the pecorino. Toss to mix well.

Place half of the pasta in a 13-by-9-by-2-inch baking dish. Top with the eggplant. Arrange half of the mozzarella, half of the caciocavallo, and half of the remaining pecorino over the eggplant. Spread the remaining pasta over the cheeses. Top with the remaining mozzarella, caciocavallo, and pecorino. Drizzle with the extra-virgin olive oil and sprinkle with the bread crumbs. Bake until the cheese melts and the top becomes crispy, about 15 minutes.

# SMALL PASTA TUBES AND LAMB SAUCE WITH AGED RICOTTA

*Pennette con Ricotta Salata*

SERVES 6

*The Italian word* ricotta *means "recooked," which describes how the cheese is made. In Basilicata, leftover whey from cheese made with cow's milk is processed again to make ricotta. Ricotta salata is aged until firm, which allows the cheese to be shaved or grated for pasta. Firm yet moist, sweet yet salty, ricotta salata is a variable cheese, depending on how long it is aged.*

Heat the olive oil in a large sauté pan over medium-high heat. Add the lamb, peperoncino, marjoram, and thyme. Cook until the lamb becomes browned and crispy, about 8 minutes. Add the onion and garlic and cook 2 minutes. Add 1/2 teaspoon of the salt and the pepper. Add the wine and cook until evaporated, about 3 minutes. Place the tomatoes in a medium bowl and break up with your hands. Add to the pan. Bring to a boil, reduce the heat, and simmer 30 minutes.

Bring 5 quarts of water and the remaining 5 teaspoons of salt to a boil in a large stockpot over high heat. Add the pasta and cook until al dente. Transfer to a colander to drain. Add to the pan with the lamb sauce. Add the grated ricotta salata and toss to mix well. Drizzle with the extra-virgin olive oil and top with the shaved ricotta salata.

1/2 cup olive oil

3/4 pound lamb stew meat

1 dried peperoncino, broken into small pieces

1 teaspoon chopped fresh marjoram

1 teaspoon chopped fresh thyme

1/4 cup diced onion

2 garlic cloves, chopped

5 1/2 teaspoons sea salt

1/4 teaspoon freshly ground pepper

1/3 cup dry white wine

One 28-ounce can whole peeled tomatoes with their juice

1 pound dry pennette

1/2 cup freshly grated ricotta salata

2 tablespoons extra-virgin olive oil

1/4 cup shaved ricotta salata

## ROASTED PEPPERS AND CLAMS WITH PASTA STRANDS
*Spaghetti alla Lucana*

◎

SERVES 6

This dish reflects the cuisine of Basilicata—once a very impoverished region—which relies heavily on the vegetables grown in the area, including bell peppers. In this recipe, the peppers are roasted to impart a smoky, sweet taste, which complements the salty taste of the clams. Lucania is the original Latin name for Basilicata. The Roman emperor Augustus chose the Latin name in honor of the Lucani, conquerors of the area in the middle of the fifth century B.C.

Preheat the broiler.

To prepare the clams: Heat the olive oil in a large, high-sided sauté pan over high heat. Add the clams, garlic, and parsley. Quickly squeeze the lemon over the clams, then add it to the pan. Add the wine and a pinch of pepper. Cover and bring to a boil. Cook until the clams begin to open, 1 to 2 minutes. Be careful not to overcook. Spread on a baking sheet to cool. Strain the liquid into a medium bowl and reserve. Remove the clams from their shells by gently scraping with a small spoon. Reserve the empty shells.

Put the shells in a large stockpot. Add 5 quarts of water and the 5 teaspoons of salt; bring to a boil over high heat. Reduce the heat and simmer 30 minutes.

Brush the bell peppers with 1 tablespoon of the olive oil. Put in an ovenproof skillet and place under the broiler. Cook until black on all sides, 8 to 10 minutes, turning frequently; don't overcook. Let cool. Peel the peppers and discard the seeds, stems, and skin. Cut lengthwise into thin strips.

Heat the remaining 1/3 cup of olive oil in a large sauté pan over medium-high heat. Add the garlic, peperoncini, and half of the parsley. Cook 2 to 3 minutes. Add the wine and cook until nearly evaporated, about 5 minutes. Add the roasted peppers, the clams, and their reserved liquid. Bring to a boil and season with salt.

Remove the clam shells from the water with tongs or a skimmer. Add enough water so that you have 5 quarts again. Bring to a boil over high heat. Add the pasta and cook until al dente. Transfer to a colander to drain. Add to the pan with the clams. Add the remaining parsley. Toss to mix well. Drizzle with the extra-virgin olive oil and season with pepper.

*For the clams:*

1/4 cup olive oil

2 1/2 pounds small, fresh clams, well rinsed (see Note on page 72)

3 garlic cloves, chopped

1 tablespoon chopped fresh Italian parsley

1/2 lemon

1/2 cup dry white wine

Freshly ground pepper

5 teaspoons sea salt, plus extra for seasoning

1 medium yellow bell pepper

1 medium red bell pepper

1/3 cup plus 1 tablespoon olive oil

3 garlic cloves, sliced

1 1/2 dried peperoncini, broken into small pieces

2 tablespoons chopped fresh Italian parsley

1/2 cup dry white wine

1 pound dry spaghetti

2 tablespoons extra-virgin olive oil

Freshly ground pepper

SERVES 6

⅓ cup plus 3 tablespoons olive oil

1 pound mild Italian sausage, crumbled

1 small sweet onion, such as Maui, diced

1 ½ dried peperoncini, broken into small pieces

2 garlic cloves, smashed

5 ½ teaspoons sea salt

½ cup dry red wine

One 28-ounce can whole peeled tomatoes with their juice

1 pound dry rigatoni

1 cup smoked or plain ricotta

½ cup freshly grated Pecorino Romano

1 tablespoon plus 1 teaspoon chopped fresh oregano

3 tablespoons extra-virgin olive oil

¼ teaspoon freshly ground pepper

An Italian salumeria, or sausage shop, is like a candy store for meat lovers. Sausages in every length and width hang from the ceiling, beckoning the hungry. Calabria is considered home to some of the best-tasting pork—because the pigs are still grazed in small, traditional farms—and therefore the most delicious pork sausages. Salsiccia Calabrese, a well-known spicy sausage, and coppa, a firm sausage, are both relatively easy to find in the United States and are wonderful examples of Calabria's renowned pork products.

Heat 3 tablespoons of the olive oil in a large sauté pan over medium-high heat. Add the sausage and cook until it begins to brown, about 5 minutes. Transfer to a colander to drain any excess oil. Return to the sauté pan and heat over medium-high heat. Add the remaining ⅓ cup of olive oil, the onion, peperoncini, and garlic. Cook until the onion is soft, 3 to 5 minutes. Add ½ teaspoon of the salt. Add the wine and cook until evaporated, about 3 minutes. Put the tomatoes in a medium bowl and break up with your hands. Add to the pan and bring to a boil; reduce the heat to low and simmer 25 to 30 minutes.

Bring 5 quarts of water and the remaining 5 teaspoons of salt to a boil in a large stockpot over high heat. Add the pasta and cook until al dente. Transfer to a colander to drain. Add to the pan with the sausage sauce. Add the ricotta, pecorino, and oregano. Toss to mix well. Drizzle with the extra-virgin olive oil and season with the pepper.

## Cavatelli con Braciolette

———————————————⊙———————————————

SERVES 6

Braciole are a great example of regional culinary differences. In the north, braciole refers to a cut of meat, including pork cut like a chop with the bone in. In the south, it is a meat roll stuffed with a filling and braised in a sauce. In Italy pasta and meat are typically served as separate courses. This recipe—created by Puglia farmers—combines the two courses into one savory dish.

To prepare the meat rolls: Combine the parsley and garlic in a small bowl. Add the olive oil and nutmeg and mix well. Add the pecorino and stir to combine. Arrange the meat slices on a flat work surface. Sprinkle with the salt and pepper. Spread the garlic mixture equally over the slices of meat. Top each one with a slice of pancetta. Roll into a tight cylinder and secure with a toothpick at the end and in the middle.

Place the tomatoes in a medium bowl and break up with your hands. Set aside. Place the flour in a shallow bowl. Heat the olive oil in a large sauté pan over medium-high heat. Toss the meat rolls in the flour and coat completely. Add the rolls to the pan and cook, turning the rolls, until browned on all sides. Add the onion, peperoncino, and garlic. Cook until the onion is soft, about 5 minutes. Season with salt. Add the wine and cook until nearly evaporated, 1 to 2 minutes.

Add the tomatoes to the pan. Add the basil and bring the mixture to a boil. Reduce the heat to low, cover, and cook 2 hours, stirring every 10 to 15 minutes. If the liquid begins to evaporate, add a small amount of hot water to keep the meat moist.

Bring 5 quarts of water and the 5 teaspoons of salt to a boil in a large stockpot over high heat. Add the pasta and cook until al dente. Transfer to a colander to drain.

Remove the meat rolls from the pan. Add the pasta, extra-virgin olive oil, and pecorino. Toss to mix well. Transfer to a serving platter. Arrange the meat rolls on top of the pasta and sprinkle with the parsley.

For the meat rolls:

3 tablespoons chopped fresh Italian parsley

3 garlic cloves, minced

1 tablespoon olive oil

1/4 teaspoon ground nutmeg

3/4 cup freshly grated Pecorino Romano

1 pound pork loin or beef top round, cut into 6 slices, each pounded 1/8 inch thick

1/2 teaspoon sea salt

1/4 teaspoon freshly ground pepper

3 ounces thinly sliced pancetta, cut in half

One 28-ounce can whole peeled tomatoes with their juice

Flour for dredging

1/3 cup olive oil

1/2 cup diced onion

1 dried peperoncino, broken into small pieces

1 garlic clove, smashed

5 teaspoons sea salt, plus extra for seasoning

1/2 cup dry red wine

6 fresh medium basil leaves, torn into small pieces

1 pound dry cavatelli

2 tablespoons extra-virgin olive oil

1/4 cup freshly grated Pecorino Romano

1 teaspoon chopped fresh Italian parsley

# Fresh Pasta "Handkerchiefs" with Mussels, Beans, and Tomatoes

*Fazzoletti con Cozze e Fagioli*

SERVES 6

¼ cup dry borlotti or white beans, soaked in water overnight

½ teaspoon sea salt

1 recipe Basic Pasta (page 21)

For the mussels:

⅓ cup olive oil

1 tablespoon fresh Italian parsley

1 garlic clove, smashed

2 ½ pounds black mussels, well rinsed and debearded

½ cup dry white wine

⅓ cup olive oil

3 dried peperoncini, broken into small pieces

3 garlic cloves, sliced lengthwise

3 tablespoons chopped fresh Italian parsley

1 cup peeled and seeded plum tomatoes, cut lengthwise into 6 strips

5 ½ teaspoons sea salt

2 tablespoons extra-virgin olive oil

*Italians are bean eaters. The taste for beans probably originated during less prosperous times, but the combination of beans and pasta has remained a national favorite. In this classic dish of Puglia, mussels are paired with borlotti beans.*

Rinse the beans and place in a large saucepan. Cover with twice as much water. Bring to a boil over medium-high heat. Reduce the heat to low and simmer until the beans are tender, about 1 hour. Add the salt.

Prepare the pasta as directed on page 21. Let sit 30 minutes.

Roll out the pasta dough into two 48-inch sheets as described in steps 1 to 6 under "To roll out strands and ribbons" on page 22. Cut each sheet crosswise into eight 6-inch lengths. Cut each of these in half lengthwise. Cut each strip into 4 triangles, cutting from corner to corner on the diagonal. Let sit 20 minutes before moving. Transfer to a flour-dusted platter and sprinkle lightly with flour. Let dry at least 2 hours, moving occasionally to prevent sticking and add body to the triangles, so they will look like folded handkerchiefs.

To prepare the mussels: Heat a large, high-sided sauté pan over medium-high heat. Add the olive oil, parsley, and garlic. Add the mussels and cover. Cook about 1 minute, shaking the pan back and forth once. Add the wine, cover, and cook until the mussels begin to open, 2 to 3 minutes. Do not overcook. Transfer to a baking sheet to cool. Remove the mussels from the shells by gently scraping with a small spoon. Strain the liquid from the pan into a bowl and reserve.

Heat the ⅓ cup olive oil in a large sauté pan over medium-high heat. Add the peperoncini, garlic, and half of the parsley. Cook until the garlic becomes soft, 3 to 5 minutes. Add the tomatoes and ½ teaspoon of the salt. Cook until all of the liquid is completely evaporated, about 3 minutes. Add the beans and then the reserved strained liquid from the mussels. Bring to a boil. Cook until reduced by half, about 3 minutes. Reduce the heat to low and keep warm while the pasta is cooking.

Bring 5 quarts of water and the remaining 5 teaspoons of salt to a boil in a large stockpot over high heat. Add the pasta and cook 1 minute. Transfer to a colander to drain. Add to the pan with the tomato sauce. Add the mussels, extra-virgin olive oil, and remaining parsley. Toss to mix well.

# "LITTLE EARS" OF PASTA
## WITH RAPINI, ANCHOVIES, AND GARLIC
### Orecchiette con Cime di Rapa

◉

SERVES 6

*Orecchiette, a pasta shaped to hold chunky sauces, originated in Puglia. This dish is best made during spring and summer, when rapini (broccoli rabe) is in season.*

Mince 2 of the garlic cloves and smash the remaining one. Set aside. Cut the rapini florets away from the stalks and set aside. Cut each stalk in half lengthwise and cut off the tough bottoms. Reserve the bottoms. Cut the stalks into 1-inch pieces.

Bring 5 quarts of water and the 5 teaspoons of salt to a boil in a large stockpot over high heat. Add the florets and count to 5. Remove the florets from the water with a slotted spoon or skimmer. Cut into 1/2-inch pieces, leaving the very tops of the florets intact.

Add the reserved bottoms of the stalks to the water. Bring to a boil and simmer 20 minutes.

While the rapini bottoms are cooking, heat 2 tablespoons of the olive oil in a large sauté pan over medium-high heat. Add the smashed garlic and half of the peperoncini. Cook until the garlic is soft, 1 to 2 minutes. Add the raw 1-inch pieces of rapini stalks. Cook 1 minute. Add the wine and cook until nearly evaporated, about 5 min-

utes. Transfer to the bowl of a food processor and purée. Set aside.

Heat the remaining 1/3 cup of olive oil in a large sauté pan over medium-high heat. Add the anchovy, minced garlic, and remaining peperoncini. Reduce the heat to low and cook 10 minutes. Add the rapini purée and floret pieces; cook 2 to 3 minutes.

Remove the rapini bottoms from the water and discard. Add the pasta and cook until al dente. Transfer to a colander to drain. Add to the pan with the anchovy mixture. Add the pecorino and extra-virgin olive oil. Toss to mix well.

3 garlic cloves

2 bunches rapini
(about 2 pounds)

5 teaspoons sea salt

1/3 cup plus 2 tablespoons
olive oil

2 dried peperoncini,
broken into small pieces

1/4 cup dry white wine

2 anchovy fillets, minced

1 pound orecchiette

1/2 cup freshly grated
Pecorino Romano

2 tablespoons
extra-virgin olive oil

ON THE ISLANDS

Italy counts roughly the same number of islands as it does regions in its territory. The two largest, Sardegna and Sicilia, are regions unto themselves, separated by mere miles of Mediterranean Sea. Simple and unspoiled, these two distinctive places have entirely different cultures, but share a common history, expressed in the cuisine of each island.

Sardegna's mountainous, rough terrain is dotted with sheep that provide both the lamb and the cheese that are found in many of the region's classic pasta dishes. Some say Sardegna is more Greek and Arabian than Italian. Given the prominence of lamb and saffron in Sardegna's cuisine—most likely due to the influence of the Greeks and Phoenicians—this is easy to believe.

Sicilia, called "the garden" by the Arabs and "the granary" by the Romans, comprises gentle countryside—rolling green hills and blue, blue coastlines. Wild fennel, orange trees, and olive groves share the land with vineyards and fields of cultivated vegetables, which dominate the Sicilian diet.

It's not surprising that the cuisines of both islands make use of the seafood that is so abundant in the surrounding waters. Sardegna and Sicilia are home to several large fishing ports, and there seems to be a fisherman catching his dinner wherever you go. Many residents of the inland towns buy the day's catch from the fishermen who transfer their load from boat to truck and then set up shop in the town square, offering a range of choices, such as fresh sardines, octopus, squid, swordfish, and tuna.

Sheep's milk cheese, especially fresh ricotta in Sicilia, is a fairly common ingredient found in both the sweet and savory dishes of the islands. Locally produced pecorino is used more than the cow's milk cheeses found in the north. When cheese wasn't available during hard times, ingenious Sicilians used toasted bread crumbs to give the illusion of grated cheese. This technique is still used today—see Pasta N'caciata (page 165).

Semolina, believed to have been introduced to Sicilia by travelers crossing the Mediterranean Sea, was once a very important crop, supplying most of the flour used for making pasta. It is still used almost exclusively for making both the dried and fresh pasta eaten in this region.

I selected the recipes for this chapter to give you the opportunity to taste the sea, the gardens, and the culinary history of these beautiful and bountiful regions.

SARDEGNA

SICILIA

## SARDEGNA

*Spaghettini all'Aragosta* 151
THIN PASTA STRANDS WITH
LOBSTER SAUCE

*Spaghetti con la Bottarga* 152
DRIED TUNA ROE SHAVED INTO
AN AROMATIC SAUCE AND
TOSSED WITH PASTA STRANDS

*Culurgionis di Patate* 153
POTATO AND CHEESE–
FILLED RAVIOLI

*Malloreddus di Campidano* 155
SAFFRON AND SEMOLINA
DUMPLINGS IN A SAFFRON,
SAUSAGE, AND LAMB SAUCE

## SICILIA

*Involtini alle Melanzane con Spaghetti* 156
PASTA STRANDS ROLLED IN EGGPLANT
SLICES WITH A TOMATO-BASIL SAUCE

*Spaghetti ai Ricci di Mare* 158
SEA URCHIN WITH PASTA STRANDS

*Spaghettini con Pesce Spada* 159
SWORDFISH, SAUTÉED EGGPLANT,
AND MINT WITH THIN PASTA STRANDS

*Ravioli alle Melanzane* 160
FRESH PASTA STUFFED WITH AN
EGGPLANT-PECORINO FILLING

*Penne con Cavolfiore* 163
CAULIFLOWER, GOLDEN RAISINS,
AND PINE NUTS TOSSED WITH
SMALL PASTA TUBES

*Pasta N'caciata* 165
PASTA, HAM, EGGS,
AND CHEESE BAKED BETWEEN
EGGPLANT SLICES

*Linguine al Pesto Trapanese* 167
PASTA RIBBONS DRESSED
WITH A ROASTED TOMATO
AND BASIL PESTO

*Fettuccine con Zucchine alla Siciliana* 168
SAUTÉED ZUCCHINI AND PASTA RIBBONS

# THIN PASTA STRANDS WITH LOBSTER SAUCE
## *Spaghettini all'Aragosta*

SERVES 6

When it comes to lobster, Sardegna is Italy's Maine. These briny creatures are abundant in the seas surrounding the island. Although black truffles are not indigenous to the region, I once added a small amount to this dish and it was so delicious, I have included it ever since.

To prepare the lobster: Set the lobsters on a cutting board, shell-side up. Make an insertion in the middle of the head with a sharp chef's knife and cut the body in half, lengthwise. Cut off the claws. Break the claws by hitting the top of the claws with the back of a heavy knife. Heat the olive oil in a large sauté pan and add half of the lobster bodies, shell-side up, and all of the claws. Add the garlic and cook until the lobster meat begins to turn brown and crispy, 2 to 3 minutes. Transfer the lobster bodies to a bowl, leaving the claws in the pan. Add the remaining lobster bodies and cook until the lobster meat begins to turn brown and crispy, 2 to 3 minutes. Transfer to the bowl. Let cool slightly. Separate the meat from the shells, reserving the liquid. Chop the meat into large pieces. Cut the shells into small pieces.

To make the broth: Heat the olive oil in a large sauté pan over medium-high heat. Add the garlic, onion, celery, carrots, and parsley; cook 2 minutes. Add the lobster shells and cook until dry, 1 to 2 minutes. Remove from the heat. Add the brandy and light with a match. Return to the heat. Carefully swirl the pan to mix the ingredients and cook off the alcohol. Cook until nearly evaporated, 1 to 2 minutes. Add the wine when the flame is extinguished and cook until evaporated, about 5 minutes. Add the water and bring to a boil. Reduce the heat and simmer 30 minutes. Strain through a fine sieve or food mill to eliminate the shells, squeezing them to remove all of the liquid. Return the broth to the sauté pan and bring to a boil over medium-high heat. Cook until reduced to 1 cup, about 5 minutes. Pour the broth into a bowl and wipe out the sauté pan.

To make the sauce: Heat the olive oil in the pan over medium-high heat. Add the garlic, onion, and peperoncino. Increase the heat to high and cook 2 minutes. Add the basil, tomatoes, and salt; cook 3 to 5 minutes. Transfer to the bowl of a food processor and coarsely chop for 5 seconds. Return to the pan, add the broth, and bring to a boil. Cook 2 to 3 minutes. Add the lobster meat and bring to a boil. Reduce the heat to low and keep warm while the pasta is cooking.

Bring 5 quarts of water and the 5 teaspoons of salt to a boil in a large stockpot over high heat. Add the pasta and cook until al dente. Transfer to a colander to drain. Add to the sauté pan with lobster sauce. Add the truffle, if desired, extra-virgin olive oil, parsley, and pepper. Toss to mix well.

Note: For a dramatic presentation, leave the shell and meat of the tail portion whole for the garnish, and follow the directions for the remaining shells and meat.

For the lobster:

Three 1 ¼-pound live lobsters

⅓ cup olive oil

2 garlic cloves, smashed

For the broth:

¼ cup olive oil

2 garlic cloves, smashed

⅓ cup diced onion

⅓ cup diced celery

⅓ cup diced carrots

3 tablespoons chopped fresh Italian parsley

⅓ cup brandy

1 cup dry white wine

5 cups water

For the sauce:

½ cup olive oil

2 garlic cloves, smashed

3 tablespoons diced white onion

½ dried peperoncino, broken into small pieces

3 tablespoons fresh basil leaves, torn into small pieces

1 ½ pounds cherry tomatoes, halved

½ teaspoon sea salt

5 teaspoons sea salt

1 pound dry spaghettini

1 black truffle, thinly sliced (optional)

2 tablespoons extra-virgin olive oil

1 tablespoon chopped fresh Italian parsley

½ teaspoon freshly ground pepper

## DRIED TUNA ROE SHAVED INTO AN AROMATIC SAUCE AND TOSSED WITH PASTA STRANDS

*Spaghetti con la Bottarga*

⊚

SERVES 6

⅓ cup freshly
grated bottarga

2 tablespoons
sliced bottarga

¼ cup plus 3 tablespoons
olive oil

¾ cup fresh
white bread crumbs

3 garlic cloves, chopped

½ dried peperoncino,
broken into small pieces

1 tablespoon chopped fresh
Italian parsley

2 tablespoons sea salt

1 pound dry spaghetti

¼ cup extra-virgin
olive oil

Freshly ground pepper

Bottarga is a delicacy from Sardegna. The roe sac of mullet or tuna is dried to create a concentrated, salty taste of the sea. Although bottarga made from mullet roe may be more difficult to find than that made from tuna roe, it has a superior taste and is well worth the search. Bottarga is available at many Italian specialty stores.

Place the grated and sliced bottarga in a bowl and add ¼ cup of the olive oil. Set aside.

Heat the remaining 3 tablespoons of olive oil in a large sauté pan over medium-high heat. Add the bread crumbs, garlic, and peperoncino. Cook until the bread crumbs become crispy, about 3 minutes, stirring continuously to prevent burning. Add the parsley and 1 teaspoon of the salt.

Bring 5 quarts of water and the remaining 5 teaspoons of salt to a boil in a large stockpot over high heat. Add the pasta and cook until al dente. Transfer to a colander to drain, reserving ½ cup of the cooking water. Add the pasta to the pan with the bread crumb mixture. Add the bottarga and toss to mix well. If the pasta sticks together, add the reserved water, ¼ cup at a time. Add the extra-virgin olive oil and toss again to mix well. Season with pepper.

# POTATO AND CHEESE-FILLED RAVIOLI
## *Culurgionis di Patate*

---

*Every town in Sardegna has its own version of this ravioli, which gains its regional flair from the use of pecorino as the main ingredient of the filling. The pecorino is sometimes combined with Swiss chard, sometimes with potatoes. While this dish is not commonly served with tomato sauce, I tasted it this way on a visit to Sardegna and prefer it. There is even a sweet version of culurgionis filled with ricotta, eggs, and cinnamon served as a dessert.*

Preheat the oven to 450°F.

Wrap the potatoes in a double layer of aluminum foil and place in an ovenproof skillet. Bake until tender, about 45 minutes. Let cool.

In a large shallow bowl or on a flat work surface, mix together the flour and 1/2 teaspoon of the salt and shape into a mound. Make a well in the center. Add the water and beat with a fork, gradually beating a wider path and incorporating the flour in very small amounts. Continue mixing with the fork until the dough begins to resemble a dry, crumbly mixture. Transfer to a flour-dusted flat work surface and begin kneading by hand, rolling the dough sideways across the surface from hand to hand, and applying strong pressure while squeezing the dough. Knead until all of the flour is incorporated, no floury white spots remain, and the dough begins to soften and is no longer sticky, 3 to 5 minutes. Shape into a ball, cover with plastic wrap, and let sit 30 minutes. (This allows the flour to continue to absorb moisture from the water.)

Peel the potatoes and press through a potato ricer into a medium bowl. Add 1/2 cup of the pecorino, the parmigiano, and provolone. Mix well.

Melt 1/4 cup of the butter in a large sauté pan over medium-high heat. Add the sage and cook until crispy, about 5 minutes. Pour over the potato-cheese mixture and add 3/4 teaspoon of the salt; mix well. Set aside.

Roll out the pasta as described in steps 1 and 2 under "To roll out sheets" on page 22. Brush each 48-inch sheet with some of the beaten egg and cut into 4-inch circles with a fluted cookie cutter. Place a large mound (about 1 tablespoon) of the potato mixture on one half of each circle. Fold the other half over the filling and press to seal the edges. Arrange on a plate with the edges pointing upwards and gently flatten the bottom.

Pour the tomato sauce into a large sauté pan and keep warm on low heat.

Bring 5 quarts of water and 5 teaspoons of the salt to a boil in a large stockpot over high heat. Add the culurgionis and cook until they rise to the top, about 5 minutes. Transfer to a colander to drain.

Divide the tomato sauce among 6 plates. Arrange the culurgionis over the pasta sauce and sprinkle with the remaining 2 tablespoons of pecorino. Melt the remaining 1/4 cup of butter in a medium sauté pan. Add the remaining 3/4 teaspoon of salt. Spoon over the culurgionis and sprinkle with pepper.

---

*2 medium baking potatoes (about 1/2 pound each)*

*1 1/4 cups flour*

*2 tablespoons plus 1 teaspoon sea salt*

*1/3 cup plus 2 tablespoons water*

*1/2 cup plus 2 tablespoons freshly grated pecorino*

*1/2 cup freshly grated Parmigiano-Reggiano*

*1/4 pound provolone, cut into 1/2-inch cubes*

*1/2 cup (1 stick) unsalted butter*

*1/4 cup chopped fresh sage*

*1 egg, beaten*

*1 cup Salsa di Pomodoro (page 24)*

*Freshly ground pepper*

# SAFFRON AND SEMOLINA DUMPLINGS
## IN A SAFFRON, SAUSAGE, AND LAMB SAUCE
### Malloreddus di Campidano

◎

SERVES 6

In Italy, saffron is grown only in Sardegna and Abruzzo. It is a delicacy because the crocus from which it is harvested produces only a few pistils each, and it takes over 14,000 pistils to create one ounce of this delicate spice. This Sardinian specialty is named after the town of Campidano, a dry plain on the western coast of Sardegna valued for its agriculture.

To make the pasta: Combine the water and saffron in a small saucepan. Bring to a boil over high heat. Cook until reduced to 3/4 cup, 5 to 10 minutes. Strain through a sieve into a bowl, but do not discard the saffron threads. Set the liquid aside to cool. Chop the saffron threads into a fine dice.

Combine the semolina and salt in a wide shallow bowl or on a flat work surface and shape into a mound. Make a well in the center and add the diced saffron and reserved liquid. Beat with a fork, gradually beating a wider path and incorporating the semolina in small amounts until it is completely incorporated. Knead the pasta, using your hands, and adding semolina as needed, until the pasta no longer sticks to your hands.

Roll the dough into a 5-inch-long cylinder and then 5 longer cylinders as directed in the Step-by-Step Guide for Shaping Dumplings on page 23. Cut into 3/4-inch pieces. Press each piece against the tines on the back of a fork while gently rolling it down. Transfer to a flour-dusted plate with a spatula.

Heat the 1/3 cup of olive oil in a large sauté pan over medium-high heat. Add the garlic and onion; cook 1 minute. Add the sausage and lamb and cook until browned, about 5 minutes. Add the thyme and bay leaf and cook 5 minutes. Add the wine and cook until nearly evaporated, about 5 minutes. Add the tomatoes, basil, saffron threads, and a pinch of salt and pepper. Bring to a boil, reduce the heat, and simmer 45 minutes.

Bring 5 quarts of water and the 5 teaspoons of salt to a boil in a large stockpot over high heat. Add the pasta and cook until al dente, 5 to 10 minutes. Transfer to a colander to drain. Add to the pan with the sausage and lamb sauce. Add the pecorino and toss to mix well.

For the pasta:

2 cups water

1 teaspoon saffron threads

2 cups semolina

1/2 teaspoon sea salt

1/3 cup olive oil

2 garlic cloves, minced

1/2 cup diced white onion

1/2 pound mild Italian sausage, crumbled

1/2 pound lean lamb stew meat, cut into 1/2-inch cubes

1 teaspoon fresh thyme leaves

1 bay leaf

1 cup dry white wine

One 28-ounce can whole peeled tomatoes with their juice

8 fresh medium basil leaves, torn into small pieces

1 scant teaspoon saffron threads

5 teaspoons sea salt, plus extra for seasoning

Freshly ground pepper

1/4 cup freshly grated Pecorino Romano

# PASTA STRANDS ROLLED IN EGGPLANT SLICES WITH A TOMATO-BASIL SAUCE

### Involtini alle Melanzane con Spaghetti

◉

SERVES 6

Sicilia's warm climate encourages prolific crops of eggplant in a variety of shapes, from round globes to small, slender cylinders. As a result, eggplant is a common ingredient in Sicilian cuisine, including a variety of pasta dishes, such as this one.

**3 large eggplants (about 1 pound each)**

**5 teaspoons sea salt, plus extra for seasoning**

**2 cups Salsa di Pomodoro (page 24)**

**1 ½ cups vegetable oil**

**¾ pound dry spaghetti**

**¾ cup freshly grated Pecorino Romano**

**Freshly ground pepper**

**¾ cup grated ricotta salata (see headnote on page 135)**

**18 fresh medium basil leaves**

**1 tablespoon extra-virgin olive oil**

Preheat the oven to 450°F.

Trim a thin slice (about ⅛ inch) of the skin off two sides of each eggplant to make them flat. Discard the trimmings. Cut each eggplant lengthwise into six ¼-inch-thick slices. Arrange the slices in a single layer on a paper towel–lined plate. Sprinkle generously with salt and let sit at least 1 hour to eliminate any excess moisture.

Pour half the tomato sauce into the bottom of a 13-by-9-by-2-inch baking dish. Pour the remaining sauce into a large sauté pan and heat over medium heat.

Heat the vegetable oil in a large sauté pan over medium-high heat. Pat both sides of each eggplant slice dry with paper towels and add to the oil. Cook until browned and crispy, about 5 minutes, turning once after 2 to 3 minutes. Transfer to a paper towel–lined plate to absorb any excess oil. Let cool.

Bring 5 quarts of water and the 5 teaspoons of salt to a boil in a large stockpot over high heat. Cook just until the spaghetti becomes pliable, removing it before it becomes al dente, about 4 to 5 minutes. Transfer to a colander to drain. Add to the pan with the tomato sauce. Add the pecorino and a pinch of salt and pepper; toss to mix well.

Arrange the 18 eggplant slices on a flat work surface. Divide the pasta into 18 portions. Arrange each portion on the top of an eggplant slice by carefully curling the ends towards the center of the slice, so that they don't hang over the edge. Roll each eggplant slice around the little package of pasta. Arrange in the baking dish, with the exposed end of the eggplant slice on the bottom. Sprinkle the ricotta salata evenly over the tops of the eggplant bundles and bake until heated through, about 10 minutes. Top each eggplant bundle with a basil leaf and drizzle with the extra-virgin olive oil.

### Eggplant

A member of the nightshade family (which includes potatoes, tomatoes, sweet peppers, and chile peppers), eggplant was once thought to cause insanity. It was also believed to be poisonous by some, but neither notion turned out to be true. There is equal confusion about how it made its way from India, where it originates, to Sicilia, where it was introduced to the kitchen gardens in the 1300s. It has since been variously used as an ornamental plant, for medicinal purposes, and as an ingredient in a wide variety of dishes, from pasta to caponata, a vegetable relish.

◎

SERVES 6

*Fresh sea urchin is very flavorful and requires little preparation; it is a perfect food for eating right out of the shell. In fact, until noncommercial harvesting of sea urchin was forbidden due to their slow reproduction capabilities, Sicilian fishermen would haul sea urchin onto the decks of their boats, cut open the large outer shell, extract the fish, and sauté it in its juice right there. It is best to buy sea urchin whole in order to use the flavorful juices, but it is easier to buy it cleaned from a fishmonger or Japanese sushi restaurant.*

1 cup (about 6 ounces) sea urchin (see Note)

2 tablespoons olive oil

3 garlic cloves, minced

1 dried peperoncino

2 tablespoons chopped fresh parsley

5 teaspoons sea salt, plus extra for seasoning

1 pound dry spaghetti

Freshly ground pepper

1/3 cup extra-virgin olive oil

Cut the sea urchin in half. Transfer one half to the bowl of a food processor and purée. Cut the remaining half into thin slices, then cut in half again, lengthwise.

Heat the olive oil in a large sauté pan over medium-high heat. Add the garlic and peperoncino. Cook until the garlic is soft, 2 to 3 minutes. Add half of the parsley and a pinch of salt.

Bring 5 quarts of water and the 5 teaspoons of salt to a boil in a large stockpot over high heat. Add the pasta and cook until al dente. Transfer to a colander to drain, reserving 1 cup of the water. Add the pasta to the pan with the parsley and garlic mixture. Add the puréed sea urchin. Add the remaining parsley and a pinch of pepper. Toss to mix well, adding the reserved cooking water as needed (if using whole sea urchin, add its juice), the remaining sliced sea urchin, and the extra-virgin olive oil. Toss to mix well.

Note: If you prefer to use whole sea urchin, purchase 6. Hold each sea urchin with thick gloves or a heavy towel while cutting the shell in half with scissors. Collect the liquid. Extract only the orange parts of the fish and cook according to the directions above. Add the liquid from the sea urchins to the pasta instead of the reserved cooking water.

# Swordfish, Sautéed Eggplant, and Mint with Thin Pasta Strands
## *Spaghettini con Pesce Spada*

*The quantity and assortment of swordfish cuts in Sicilia is unlike any others I've seen. Once when I was on a trip to Sicilia, a stack of fresh swordfish caught my eye and I took out my camera to take a photograph. As I tried to take the picture, I was chased away by the fishmonger. I was a bit surprised because swordfish is so abundant; I only had to walk to the next shop to see a nearly identical display. In this recipe, the rich taste and firm texture of the swordfish complement the eggplant and mint.*

Arrange the eggplant in a single layer on a paper towel–lined plate. Sprinkle a generous amount of salt over the eggplant and let sit at least 1 hour to eliminate any excess moisture.

Pat the eggplant dry with a paper towel. Place in a bowl and add the flour. Toss to coat evenly. Heat the vegetable oil in a large sauté pan over medium-high heat. Shake any excess flour off the eggplant and add to the pan. Cook until browned and crispy, about 5 minutes. Transfer to a paper towel–lined plate to absorb any excess oil. Set aside. Wipe out the pan and return it to the stove.

Heat 1/3 cup of the olive oil in the pan over medium-high heat. Add the garlic and cook until light brown, 1 to 2 minutes. Add the tomatoes, half of the mint, and a pinch of salt and pepper. Bring to a boil. Reduce the heat to low and simmer 25 minutes.

Heat the remaining 2 tablespoons of olive oil in a medium sauté pan over medium-high heat. Add the swordfish and sprinkle with a generous amount of salt and pepper. Cook until browned, 5 to 10 minutes. Drain the oil from the pan. Add the wine and cook until the wine evaporates and the fish is evenly browned, about 10 minutes. Add to the tomato mixture. Bring to a boil. Reduce the heat to low and keep warm while the pasta is cooking.

Bring 5 quarts of water and the 5 teaspoons of salt to a boil in a large stockpot over high heat. Add the pasta and cook until al dente. Transfer to a colander to drain. Add to the pan with the tomato-swordfish sauce. Add the eggplant, extra-virgin olive oil, and remaining mint. Toss to mix well.

---

2 medium Japanese eggplants, cut into 1/2-inch cubes

5 teaspoons sea salt, plus extra for seasoning

Flour for dredging

1 cup vegetable oil

1/3 cup plus 2 tablespoons olive oil

2 garlic cloves, minced

One 28-ounce can whole peeled tomatoes, cut lengthwise into 1/2-inch strips, with their juice

1/3 cup fresh mint leaves, chopped

Freshly ground pepper

3/4 pound swordfish fillet, skinned and cut into 1-inch cubes

1/2 cup white wine

1 pound dry spaghetti

3 tablespoons extra-virgin olive oil

# Fresh Pasta Stuffed with an Eggplant-Pecorino Filling
## Ravioli alle Melanzane

**For the filling:**

2 large eggplants (about 1 pound each), halved and meat-side scored

2 teaspoons sea salt

1 tablespoon olive oil

½ cup freshly grated Pecorino Romano

½ cup freshly grated Parmigiano-Reggiano

½ teaspoon freshly ground pepper

**For the pasta:**

1 ¼ cups all-purpose flour

½ teaspoon sea salt

¼ teaspoon ground dried peperoncino

2 large eggs at room temperature

1 teaspoon olive oil

2 cups Salsa di Pomodoro (page 24)

1 egg, beaten

5 teaspoons sea salt

2 tablespoons chopped fresh oregano

There is a common misconception that all Sicilian cuisine is spicy. While spicy food is popular here, this ravioli dish shows that even when peperoncino is included, it can be used in moderation. Because the filling in this recipe has a very subtle flavor, the dough is rolled out thinner than other stuffed pastas.

Preheat the oven to 375°F.

Arrange the eggplant in a single layer on a paper towel–lined plate. Sprinkle 1½ teaspoons of the salt over the eggplant and let sit, scored-side down, at least 1 hour to eliminate any excess moisture.

Pat the eggplant dry with a paper towel. Place in a baking dish, scored-side up, and brush with the olive oil. Bake until tender, 30 to 45 minutes. Scoop out the meat and transfer to a bowl. Add the pecorino, parmigiano, the remaining ½ teaspoon of salt, and the pepper. Mix well and season with additional salt and pepper.

To make the pasta: In a large shallow bowl or on a flat work surface, mix the flour, salt, and peperoncino together and shape into a mound. Make a well in the center. Crack the eggs into the well and add the olive oil. Beat the eggs and olive oil with a fork, gradually beating a wider path and incorporating the flour in very small amounts. Continue mixing with the fork until the pasta begins to resemble a dry, crumbly mixture. Transfer to a flour-dusted, flat work surface and begin kneading by hand, rolling the dough sideways across the surface from hand to hand, and applying strong pressure while squeezing the dough. Knead until all of the flour is incorporated,

no floury white spots remain, and the pasta begins to soften, about 10 minutes. Shape into a ball, cover with plastic wrap, and let sit 30 minutes. (This allows the flour to continue to absorb moisture from the eggs.)

Pour the tomato sauce into a large sauté pan and keep warm over low heat.

Roll out the pasta dough into two 48-inch sheets as described in steps 1 to 6 under "To roll out strands and ribbons" on page 22. Cut each sheet crosswise into four 12-inch lengths. Brush one long half of a pasta sheet with some of the egg. Arrange the eggplant filling in small mounds (about 2 teaspoons each), spacing them 3 inches apart, down the center of the egg-brushed half. Fold over the other pasta half, forming a long rectangle, and gently push the pasta down around each mound to squeeze out the air around the filling. Sprinkle lightly with flour. Cut into 2½-inch circles with a fluted pastry cutter. Repeat, filling the remaining sheets of pasta, and cutting them into circles.

Bring 5 quarts of water and the 5 teaspoons of salt to a boil in a large stockpot over high heat. Add the pasta and cook until the ravioli rise to the top, about 3 minutes. Transfer to a colander to drain. Add to the pan with the tomato sauce and gently stir to mix well. Sprinkle with the oregano and stir to combine.

# CAULIFLOWER, GOLDEN RAISINS, AND PINE NUTS
## TOSSED WITH SMALL PASTA TUBES
### *Penne con Cavolfiore*

SERVES 6

In Sicilia there is a popular cauliflower that can sometimes be found in the United States. Called Roman or Romanesca cauliflower, it is pale green, and the head is twice the size of the more common white cauliflower. Its size and flavor have inspired many dishes featuring the combination of cauliflower, raisins, and pine nuts, including this one. It is a great mix of sweet, bitter, and savory flavors.

Place the raisins in a small bowl and cover with the water. Let sit at least 15 minutes.

Bring 5 quarts of water and the 5 teaspoons of salt to a boil in a large stockpot over high heat. Add the cauliflower and cook until al dente, 2 to 3 minutes. Remove from the water with a slotted spoon or skimmer. Set aside.

Heat the olive oil in a medium saucepan over medium-high heat. Add the garlic and cook until browned, about 3 minutes. Add the onion and anchovies; cook until the onions are soft, about 5 minutes. Place the tomatoes in a medium bowl and break into small pieces using your hands. Add to the pan. Bring the mixture to a boil, reduce the heat, and simmer 20 minutes. Add the cauliflower. Drain the raisins, gently squeeze between your hands to eliminate any excess moisture, and add them to the pan. Add the pine nuts, basil, and a pinch of salt and pepper. Return the sauce to a boil, reduce the heat, and simmer 10 minutes.

Return the water in the stockpot to a boil. Add the pasta and cook until al dente. Transfer to a colander to drain. Add to the pan with the cauliflower mixture. Add the pecorino, extra-virgin olive oil, and parsley. Toss to mix well.

---

¼ cup golden raisins

½ cup warm water

5 teaspoons sea salt, plus extra for seasoning

1 small cauliflower head (about 1 ½ pounds), cut into florets

2 tablespoons olive oil

2 garlic cloves, chopped

½ small white onion, diced

4 anchovy fillets, minced

One 28-ounce can whole peeled tomatoes with their juice

3 tablespoons pine nuts

6 fresh medium basil leaves, torn into small pieces

Freshly ground pepper

1 pound dry penne

½ cup freshly grated Pecorino Romano

¼ cup extra-virgin olive oil

2 tablespoons chopped fresh Italian parsley

## PASTA, HAM, EGGS, AND CHEESE
## BAKED BETWEEN EGGPLANT SLICES
### *Pasta N'caciata*

◉

SERVES 6

My friend Anna Tasca Lanza, a native Sicilian who writes cookbooks and manages her family winery, served a dish similar to this one when my chefs and I visited her at her family estate near Vallelunga. While this recipe may take you a lot of time to prepare, it is well worth your effort. It can be assembled one day in advance.

Arrange the eggplant slices on a paper towel–lined baking sheet. Sprinkle liberally with salt. Let sit at least 30 minutes to eliminate any excess moisture.

Heat 1 tablespoon of the olive oil in a large sauté pan over medium-high heat. Add the beef, pork, and a pinch of salt. Stir to break the meat into pieces. Cook until evenly browned, 5 to 10 minutes. Add the wine and cook until nearly evaporated, about 2 minutes. Transfer the mixture to a bowl and set aside. Wipe out the pan and return it to the stove.

Heat the vegetable oil in the pan over medium-high heat. Pat the eggplant slices dry with a paper towel. Cook the eggplant in batches: Add to the pan in a single layer (about 6 to 8 slices) and cook until browned and crispy, about 2 minutes per side. Transfer to a paper towel–lined plate to absorb any excess oil. Continue until all of the eggplant is cooked, adding more oil if needed. Wipe out the pan.

Place the tomatoes in a medium bowl and break up with your hands. Set aside. Heat the remaining 1/3 cup of olive oil in the large sauté pan over medium heat. Add the onion and garlic. Cook 1 to 2 minutes. Add the basil and peperoncino and sauté 1 minute. Add the tomatoes to the pan. Add the meat mixture and a pinch of salt. Bring to a boil, reduce the heat, and simmer the mixture 25 minutes. Add the peas and cook 5 minutes. Season with salt and pepper.

Preheat the oven to 450°F.

Brush the bottom and sides of a 4-quart casserole dish, 10 inches in diameter and 3 inches high, with olive oil. Coat the bottom with the bread crumbs, discarding any extra. Select uniform eggplant slices and arrange in concentric circles on the bottom, beginning in the center and overlapping each slice. Line the side of the

(continued on next page)

4 to 5 large Japanese eggplants (about 2 pounds total), cut lengthwise into 1/4-inch-thick slices

5 teaspoons sea salt, plus extra for seasoning

1/3 cup plus 1 tablespoon olive oil

6 ounces ground beef

6 ounces ground pork

1/3 cup dry red wine

1 cup vegetable oil

One 28-ounce can whole peeled tomatoes with their juice

1/2 white onion, diced

3 garlic cloves, chopped

1/4 cup fresh basil leaves, torn into small pieces

1 small dried peperoncino, broken into small pieces

1 cup shelled fresh green peas

Freshly ground pepper

3 tablespoons dry bread crumbs

12 ounces dry tube pasta, such as rigatoni or penne

1/2 cup freshly grated Pecorino Romano

1/2 cup freshly grated Parmigiano-Reggiano

3 eggs, hard-boiled, peeled, and sliced

1/2 cup julienned imported Italian ham or salami

Six 1/8-inch-thick slices caciocavallo or provolone

dish with eggplant slices, beginning at the bottom. The slices should eventually hang over the edge of the dish, and the entire inside of the casserole dish should be covered. Reserve 6 slices to cover the top. (If there is additional eggplant, chop it and add to the tomato-meat sauce.)

Bring 5 quarts of water and the 5 teaspoons of salt to a boil in a large stockpot over high heat. Add the pasta and cook until al dente. Transfer to a colander to drain. Add to the pan with the tomato-meat sauce. Add the pecorino and toss to coat evenly. Season with pepper.

Pour a third of the pasta mixture into the casserole dish. Spread half of the parmigiano over the pasta. Arrange half of the egg slices over the parmigiano, and then half of the ham over the egg. Cover with half of the caciocavallo. Press down gently to compress. Repeat the layers, beginning with a third of the pasta, then the remaining parmigiano, egg, ham, and caciocavallo. Top with the remaining pasta. Arrange the remaining 6 eggplant slices over the top and fold the eggplant slices hanging over the edge over the top of the pasta. Cover with plastic wrap, and press down to compress and hold the ingredients together. Refrigerate 30 minutes. (This dish can be prepared to this point up to 1 day in advance.) Remove the plastic wrap and cover with aluminum foil. Bake 30 to 45 minutes. Remove from the oven and let sit 1 minute. Invert onto a plate.

# PASTA RIBBONS DRESSED WITH A
# ROASTED TOMATO AND BASIL PESTO
*Linguine al Pesto Trapanese*

---

SERVES 6

The town of Trápani, which juts out of the southwestern coastline of Sicily, is renowned for its abundant tomato crop. In this recipe, tomatoes are roasted and then combined with almonds in a pesto. (The Italian word pesto comes from pestare, to "smash" or "crush.") The dish tastes best with a high-quality, low-acid olive oil. If you can find a good Sicilian one, use it.

Preheat the oven to 500°F.

Arrange the tomatoes in an ovenproof sauté pan. Brush with 2 tablespoons of the olive oil and sprinkle generously with salt. Bake 15 minutes, then place under the broiler for 5 minutes.

Heat the remaining 1/2 cup of olive oil in a large sauté pan over medium heat. Add the garlic and reduce the heat to low. Cook until tender, about 15 minutes. Add 1/2 cup of the almonds. Cook until browned, 3 to 5 minutes. Remove from the heat. Add the basil and a pinch of salt and pepper. Let sit 5 minutes. Transfer to the bowl of a food processor, add the tomatoes and 1/2 cup of the pecorino cheese, and purée. Return to the sauté pan and keep warm over low heat.

Bring 5 quarts of water and the 5 teaspoons of salt to a boil in a large stockpot over high heat. Add the pasta and cook until al dente. Transfer to a colander to drain, reserving 1 cup of the cooking water. Add the pasta to the sauté pan with the pesto and toss to mix well. If the pasta sticks together because the sauce is too thick, add the reserved water, 1/4 cup at a time. Transfer to a serving dish and sprinkle with the remaining almonds and pecorino cheese.

2 pounds plum tomatoes, cored, halved, and seeded

1/2 cup plus 2 tablespoons olive oil

5 teaspoons sea salt, plus extra for seasoning

1/2 cup garlic cloves (about 2 1/2 heads)

3/4 cup sliced blanched almonds

2 cups loosely packed fresh basil leaves

Freshly ground pepper

3/4 cup freshly grated Pecorino Romano

1 pound dry linguine

# SAUTÉED ZUCCHINI AND PASTA RIBBONS
*Fettuccine con Zucchine alla Siciliana*

⊙

SERVES 6

Zucchini is a prolific crop in Sicilia, and there are more types of zucchini in the markets there than anywhere else in Italy. In this recipe, small, tender, dark green zucchini (the type that is quite abundant in the United States) is used. Because the zucchini absorbs the taste of the olive oil, do not use another type of oil.

1 ⅓ cups olive oil

9 small zucchini (about 2 pounds total), cut into ¼-inch-thick rounds

¼ cup diced onion

4 garlic cloves, smashed

5 ½ teaspoons sea salt

1 pound dry fettuccine

3 tablespoons shaved pecorino pepato (see Note)

2 tablespoons extra-virgin olive oil

Heat 1 cup of the olive oil in a large sauté pan over medium-high heat. Add two-thirds of the zucchini and cook until browned and crispy, 3 to 5 minutes. (Cook in batches if your pan is too small to fit the zucchini without crowding.) Transfer to a paper towel–lined plate with a slotted spoon. Discard the oil and wipe out the pan.

Return the pan to the stove and add the remaining ⅓ cup of olive oil. Add the onion, garlic, remaining zucchini, and ½ teaspoon of the salt. Cook until the zucchini are browned and crispy, about 5 minutes. Transfer to the bowl of a food processor and purée. Return to the pan and keep warm over low heat.

Bring 5 quarts of water and the remaining 5 teaspoons of salt to a boil in a large stockpot over high heat. Add the pasta and cook until al dente. Transfer the pasta to a colander to drain, reserving 1 cup of the cooking water. Add the pasta to the sauté pan with the zucchini purée and toss to coat evenly. If the pasta sticks together because the sauce is too thick, add the reserved cooking water, ¼ cup at a time. Add the zucchini rounds. Toss to mix well. Top with the pecorino pepato and drizzle with the extra-virgin olive oil.

Note: Pecorino pepato is a black peppercorn-studded pecorino that is commonly found in specialty cheese departments.

*In nearly every city I have visited in the United States, I have been surprised to find a delicatessen selling a wide range of Italian products, both imported and domestic. I suggest you look for such a delicatessen where you live. For more difficult-to-find items, the Internet is a great resource. You'll find a wide range of products from domestic sources, and some available directly from Italy. I do most of my shopping at a store called Draeger's in San Mateo, California. I find it carries almost every ingredient I need. If you have a gourmet-style store in your area, it, too, may offer a selection of Italian products unavailable at the supermarket.*

---

## IL FORNAIO
www.ilfornaio.com
888-ITALIAN (888-482-5426)
In various locations across the U.S.
Our signature brand of food products, from bakery goods to extra-virgin olive oil.

## CORTI BROTHERS
www.cortibrothers.com
800-509-3663
Sacramento, California
A good resource for imported Italian food products, such as pasta, olive oil, and dried porcini mushrooms.

## DEAN AND DELUCA
www.deandeluca.com
877-826-9246
In various locations across the U.S.
A wide selection of food items and housewares, such as truffles, cheeses, pots, and pans.

## DRAEGER'S
www.draegers.com
800-642-9463
In various Northern California locations
A terrific selection of gourmet food products, including dried peperoncini, meats, and seafood. They also carry a large selection of kitchenware and offer a variety of cooking classes.

## PASTA SHOP
www.rockridgemarkethall.com
510-547-4005
Berkeley, California
A reputable purveyor, the Pasta Shop offers a great selection of fresh pasta, truffles, and artisanal cheeses.

## WILLIAMS-SONOMA
www.williams-sonoma.com
800-541-2233
In various locations across the U.S.
A wonderful resource for Italian cookery products, from clay pots to fresh truffles.

*L'appetito e la salsa piu buona che ci sia.*

APPETITE IS THE BEST CONDIMENT THERE IS.

*La fame fa bone anche le verze.*

APPETITE CAN TURN PLAIN CABBAGE
INTO A TASTY MEAL.

*La volpe che non arriva al lardo dice che non é buono.*

WHEN SOMEONE CANNOT AFFORD FILET MIGNON,
HE CLAIMS IT IS NOT GOOD.

*Con le mani di un altro e facile toccare il fuoco.*

IT'S EASY TO TOUCH THE FIRE WITH
SOMEONE ELSE'S HANDS.

*La cucina del popolo e la sola esatta testimonianza
della civilitá.*

THE ONLY TRUE SIGN OF A CIVILIZATION
IS ITS CULINARY HERITAGE.

*La vita e troppo breve per bere il vino cattivo.*

LIFE IS MUCH TOO SHORT TO DRINK BAD WINE.

*Mangia e bevi come ti pare ma vestiti come si conviene.*

YOU CAN EAT AND DRINK THE WAY YOU LIKE,
AS LONG AS YOU KNOW HOW TO DRESS ACCORDINGLY.

*La fame condisce tutte le vivande.*

HUNGER SEASONS ALL FOOD.

*Del vino bisogna farne uso non abuso.*

WINE SHOULD BE USED, BUT NOT ABUSED.

*La bocca non e mai stracca se non sa da vacca.*

YOUR MOUTH SHOULD NEVER BE SO
TIRED OF EATING THAT YOU ARE UNABLE TO
FINISH YOUR MEAL WITH CHEESE.

*Finché durano pane e vino si puo ridere al destino.*

AS LONG AS YOU HAVE BREAD AND WINE,
YOU CAN LAUGH IN THE FACE OF DESTINY.

*Un pane, un fiasco e un anno——veloci se ne vanno.*

A LOAF OF BREAD, A BOTTLE OF WINE,
AND A YEAR GO VERY QUICKLY.

*Amici veri sono come meloni, di cento ne trovi due buoni.*

A TRUE FRIEND IS LIKE A CANTALOUPE,
ONLY TWO IN A HUNDRED ARE GOOD.

*Anche i pesci del re hanno spine.*

EVEN THE FISH OF A KING HAS BONES.

*Il pesce e il riso vivono nell'acqua muoiono nel vino.*

FISH AND RICE ARE BORN IN WATER AND DIE IN WINE.

*Quando la pancia è piena il cuore è contento.*

WHEN THE STOMACH IS FULL, THE HEART IS HAPPY.

ACKNOWLEDGMENTS

This book is dedicated to the memory of my mother, Maria. She started her day in the kitchen early every morning and didn't finish cooking until dinner. She cooked each meal with passion and creativity. Her energy and imagination were indefatigable. She was my hero.

My sisters, Marisa and Mara, have carried on in my mother's footsteps, preparing delicious meals for their families. They feed me such incredible food whenever I go home to Italy that I am inspired at every meal. My brother Mauro, a chef at Il Fornaio, was a great support to me as I worked to develop these recipes.

I want to thank the first chef I ever worked with, Claudio del Zotto, and his sous chef, Merino Polloni. They shared their passion, work ethic, and secrets with me for more than ten years while I worked beside them in Venice at All'Angelo.

I also feel very grateful for the opportunities I have had to work with many great chefs over the years, especially my colleagues at Il Fornaio. Their collaborative efforts have helped shape many of the recipes presented here. This book would not have been possible without Il Fornaio, and the wonderful people there. I want to thank Larry Mindel and Mike Hislop for providing an environment that inspires and nurtures creativity. Thanks also to Kristina Barnett, my assistant, who gave me invaluable support throughout the process of writing this book, and to the marketing department, especially Hilary Wolf, whose efforts and energy encouraged me at every step.

Thank you also to Lori Lyn Narlock for working with me to put my words on paper, and to Eleanor Santo Domingo for testing recipes.

I am indebted to Bill LeBlond and the staff at Chronicle Books. And I want to thank the terrific group of people who have made this book look so beautiful—photographer Michael Lamotte, food stylist Sandra Cook, prop stylist Sara Slavin, and graphic designers Michael Mabry and Margie Chu.

Abruzzo, 11, 81, 115–17, 155
Alto Adige. *See* Trentino–Alto Adige
Anchovies
    Fat Pasta Tubes in a Fresh Tomato and
      Olive Sauce, 76
    "Little Ears" of Pasta with Rapini,
      Anchovies, and Garlic, 143
    Mussels, Anchovies, and Tomatoes
      Tossed with Pasta Strands, 105
    Seafood Baked in a Tomato Sauce with
      Round Pasta Strands, 69
    Thin Pasta Strands in a Tomato-Anchovy
      Sauce, 68
Antica Pizzicheria, 81
Artichokes, 81
    Corkscrew-Shaped Pasta with Tuna,
      Artichokes, and Tomato Sauce, 114
    varieties of, 114
Arugula, Pasta Shells with Tomatoes and, 116
Asparagus
    trimming, 47
    Twisted "Twin Strands" of Pasta with a
      Four-Cheese Sauce, 47
Augustus, 137

Basic Gnocchi, 23
Basic Pasta, 21–22
Basil, 17
    A Classic Combination of Thin Pasta
      Strands and Tomato-Basil Sauce, 127
    Eggplant-Potato Dumplings Topped with
      a Tomato-Basil Sauce, 73
    Pasta Ribbons Dressed with a Roasted
      Tomato and Basil Pesto, 167
    Pasta Ribbons with Pesto, Green Beans,
      and Potatoes, 34
    Pasta Shells with Arugula and
      Tomatoes, 116
    Pasta Strands Rolled in Eggplant Slices
      with a Tomato-Basil Sauce, 156
    Potato Dumplings in a Tomato Sauce
      with Fresh Basil and Melted
      Mozzarella, 126

Basilicata, 121, 135–37
Beans
    Fresh Pasta "Handkerchiefs" with
      Mussels, Beans, and Tomatoes, 140
    Pasta Ribbons with Fava Beans,
      Pecorino, and Aged Ricotta, 100
    Pasta Ribbons with Pesto, Green Beans,
      and Potatoes, 34
Beef
    Fresh Spinach Pasta Ribbons with a
      Classic Meat Ragù, 85–86
    Meat and Spinach–Stuffed Pasta with a
      Red Wine Sauce, 46
    Pasta, Ham, Eggs, and Cheese Baked
      between Eggplant Slices, 165–66
    Pasta Stuffed with a Anise-Flavored
      Filling, 51
    Ridged Tubes with a Meat and Porcini
      Sauce Baked in a Clay Pot, 36
    Small Pasta Shells Topped with a Classic
      Meat Roll, 139
Beet-Flavored Pasta Stuffed with a Ricotta-
    Beet Filling Topped with Brown Butter
    and Poppy Seeds, 66
Bergamo, 51
Bigoli, 14, 68
    *Bigoli in Casso Pipa*, 69
    Seafood Baked in a Tomato Sauce with
      Round Pasta Strands, 69
*Boccon del Prete*, 74
Bottarga, 152
Braciole, 139
Bread crumbs, 17
Bucatini, 14
    *Bucatini alla Carbonara*, 107
    Hollow, Round Pasta Strands in a Classic
      Sauce of Pancetta and Eggs, 107
Buckwheat Noodles, Savoy Cabbage,
    Potatoes, and Fontina Cheese Baked in a
    Casserole, 48
Butter, 17
Butternut Squash Pasta Filled with a
    Butternut Squash, Parmesan, and
    Walnut Filling, 88

Cabbage (Savoy), Potatoes, Fontina
    Cheese, and Buckwheat Noodles Baked
    in a Casserole, 48
Calabria, 121, 138
Calamari, Potato Dumplings with
    Radicchio and, 77
Campania, 121, 124–34
Campidano, 155
Canal, Giovanni Antonio, 74
Canaletto Ristorante Veneto, 74
Canederli, 11
    *Canederli Tirolesi*, 59–60
    A Trio of Spinach, Mushroom, and
      Ricotta-Pancetta Dumplings in
      Chicken Stock, 59–60
Cannelloni, 12
    *Cannelloni alla Montanara*, 39–40
    cooking, 72
    making, 22
    Stuffed Pasta Tubes Baked in Béchamel
      Sauce with Mushrooms, Tomatoes,
      and Truffles, 39–40
Capers, 65
    Bow-Tie Pasta in a Smoked Salmon,
      Caper, and Brandy Cream Sauce, 54
    chopping, 54
    Fat Pasta Tubes in a Fresh Tomato and
      Olive Sauce, 76
    Sautéed Prawns with Capers, Cream,
      and Tomato Sauce over Thin Pasta
      Strands, 65
Cappellacci, 12
    Butternut Squash Pasta Filled with a
      Butternut Squash, Parmesan, and
      Walnut Filling, 88
    *Cappellacci alla Zucca*, 88
    making, 22
Casonsei, 12
    Beet-Flavored Pasta Stuffed with a
      Ricotta-Beet Filling Topped with
      Brown Butter and Poppy Seeds, 66
    *Casonsei alla Bergamasca*, 51
    *Casonsei Ampezzani*, 66
    making, 22

Pasta Stuffed with a Anise-Flavored
    Filling, 51
Cauliflower, Golden Raisins, and Pine Nuts
    Tossed with Small Pasta Tubes, 163
Cavatappi, 15
    *Cavatappi Tonno e Carciofi*, 114
    Corkscrew-Shaped Pasta with Tuna,
        Artichokes, and Tomato Sauce, 114
Cavatelli, 15
    *Cavatelli con Braciolette*, 139
    Small Pasta Shells Topped with a Classic
        Meat Roll, 139
Cheese. *See also* Mozzarella; Parmigiano-
    Reggiano; Pecorino; Ricotta; Ricotta
    salata
    caciocavallo, 134
    grana, 17
    Pasta, Ham, Eggs, and Cheese Baked
        between Eggplant Slices, 165–66
    Pasta Tubes Baked with Cheese,
        Eggplant, and Tomato Sauce, 134
    Potato and Cheese–Filled Ravioli, 153
    Potato Dumplings Baked in a
        Gorgonzola Sauce, 50
    Savoy Cabbage, Potatoes, Fontina
        Cheese, and Buckwheat Noodles
        Baked in a Casserole, 48
    Twisted "Twin Strands" of Pasta with a
        Four-Cheese Sauce, 47
Chitarrine, 11
    *Chitarrine al Sugo d'Agnello*, 117
    making, 117
    Pasta Strands with a Lamb Sauce, 117
Clams
    Fresh Pasta Baked in a Creamy Seafood
        Sauce, 71–72
    Pasta Ribbons, Mussels, Clams, Shrimp,
        Scallops, and Tomato Sauce Cooked
        in Parchment, 124
    Roasted Peppers and Clams with Pasta
        Strands, 137
    Seafood Baked in a Tomato Sauce with
        Round Pasta Strands, 69

Thin Pasta Strands with Fresh Clams
    and Garlic–White Wine Sauce, 129
    varieties of, 72, 129
Conchiglie, 15
    *Conchiglie con Rucola alla Molisana*, 116
    Pasta Shells with Arugula and
        Tomatoes, 116
Coppa, 138
Cortina, 66
Crab
    Fresh Crab with Tomatoes and Thin
        Pasta Strands, 98
    Fresh Pasta Baked in a Creamy Seafood
        Sauce, 71–72
Crespelle, 12
    *Crespelle alla Fiorentina*, 93
    Delicate Fresh Crêpes with a Spinach-
        Ricotta Filling, 93
Culurgionis, 12
    *Culurgionis di Patate*, 153
    Potato and Cheese–Filled Ravioli, 153

Dievole Winery, 97
Dry pasta. *See also individual varieties*
    cooking, 26
    fresh vs., 10
    purchasing, 18
    varieties of, 14–15, 121
Duck Sauce, Wide Pasta Ribbons in a, 97

Eggplant, 156
    Eggplant-Potato Dumplings Topped with
        a Tomato-Basil Sauce, 73
    Fresh Pasta Stuffed with an Eggplant-
        Pecorino Filling, 160
    Pasta, Ham, Eggs, and Cheese Baked
        between Eggplant Slices, 165–66
    Pasta Strands Rolled in Eggplant Slices
        with a Tomato-Basil Sauce, 156
    Pasta Tubes Baked with Cheese,
        Eggplant, and Tomato Sauce, 134
    Swordfish, Sautéed Eggplant, and Mint
        with Thin Pasta Strands, 159

Eggs, 17
    Hollow, Round Pasta Strands in a Classic
        Sauce of Pancetta and Eggs, 107
    Pasta, Ham, Eggs, and Cheese Baked
        between Eggplant Slices, 165–66
Emilia-Romagna, 12, 17, 81, 85–90
Equipment, 19
Etiquette, 65

Farfalle, 15
    Bow-Tie Pasta in a Smoked Salmon,
        Caper, and Brandy Cream Sauce, 54
    *Farfalle al Salmone*, 54
Fazzoletti, 12
    *Fazzoletti con Cozze e Fagioli*, 140
    Fresh Pasta "Handkerchiefs" with
        Mussels, Beans, and Tomatoes, 140
Fennel, 95
Fettuccine, 11, 81
    *Fettuccine con Zucchine alla Siciliana*, 168
    Sautéed Zucchini and Pasta Ribbons, 168
Fish. *See also* Anchovies; Tuna
    Bow-Tie Pasta in a Smoked Salmon,
        Caper, and Brandy Cream Sauce, 54
    Swordfish, Sautéed Eggplant, and Mint
        with Thin Pasta Strands, 159
Florence, 93
Fresh pasta. *See also individual varieties*
    Basic Pasta, 21–22
    cooking, 26
    dry vs., 10
    varieties of, 11–12
Friuli–Venezia Giulia, 12, 31, 62–65
Fusilli, 15
    Corkscrew Pasta Tossed with a Tuna
        Sauce, 108
    Corkscrew Pasta with a Sauce of
        Assorted Olives and Fresh
        Tomatoes, 94
    *Fusilli al Sugo di Olive*, 94
    *Fusilli al Tonno*, 108

Garganelli, 12
 Fresh Pasta Tubes with Porcini
  Mushrooms and Parmesan, 87
 *Garganelli ai Porcini e Parmigiano*, 87
Garlic, 17
Gemelli, 15
 *Gemelli ai Quattro Formaggi*, 47
 Twisted "Twin Strands" of Pasta with a
  Four-Cheese Sauce, 47
Genoa, 34
Gnocchetti, 11
 *Gnocchetti con Calamari e Radicchio*, 77
 making, 23
 Potato Dumplings with Calamari and
  Radicchio, 77
Gnocchi, 11
 Basic Gnocchi, 23
 *Boccon del Prete*, 74
 Eggplant-Potato Dumplings Topped with
  a Tomato-Basil Sauce, 73
 *Gnocchi alle Melanzane*, 73
 *Gnocchi Gratinati al Gorgonzola*, 50
 *Gnocchi Ripieni*, 43
 making, 23
 Potato Dumplings Baked in a
  Gorgonzola Sauce, 50
 Potato Dumplings Filled with a Sausage
  Stuffing and Topped with Tomato
  Sauce, 43
 Potato Dumplings in a Tomato Sauce
  with Fresh Basil and Melted
  Mozzarella, 126
 Ricotta-Spinach Dumplings Baked
  in a Creamy Porcini Mushroom
  Sauce, 74
 *Strangolaprieti alla Sorrentina*, 126
Grana, 17

Ham
 Fresh Pasta Ribbons Baked in a
  Cream Sauce with Sautéed Ham
  and Green Peas, 44

Ham and Ricotta Rolled in a Sheet of
 Pasta and Baked in Béchamel
 Sauce, 90
Pasta, Ham, Eggs, and Cheese Baked
 between Eggplant Slices, 165–66
Spinach Dumplings with a Ham and
 Cream Sauce, 56
Herbs, 17

*Involtini alle Melanzane con Spaghetti*, 156

Kale, black, 37

La Cisterna, 107
Lamb
 Pasta Strands with a Lamb Sauce, 117
 Saffron and Semolina Dumplings
  in a Saffron, Sausage, and Lamb
  Sauce, 155
 Small Pasta Tubes and Lamb Sauce with
  Aged Ricotta, 135
L'Antica Trattoria, 131
Lanza, Anna Tasca, 165
Lasagne, 12
 cooking, 72
 Fresh Pasta Baked in a Creamy Seafood
  Sauce, 71–72
Las Vegas, 74
Lazio, 81, 107–14
Lemons
 Prawns and Pasta Ribbons with Parsley
  Pesto, 131–32
 in southern Italy, 132
Liguria, 12, 14, 31, 34–37
Limoncello, 132
Linguine, 14
 *Linguine al Pesto Trapanese*, 167
 *Linguine Mare Chiaro al Cartoccio*, 124
 Pasta Ribbons Dressed with a Roasted
  Tomato and Basil Pesto, 167

Pasta Ribbons, Mussels, Clams, Shrimp,
 Scallops, and Tomato Sauce Cooked
 in Parchment, 124
Lobster Sauce, Thin Pasta Strands with, 151
Lombardia, 12, 31, 47–53

Malloreddus, 11
 making, 23
 *Malloreddus di Campidano*, 155
 Saffron and Semolina Dumplings
  in a Saffron, Sausage, and Lamb
  Sauce, 155
Marche, 81, 105
Molise, 81, 115–17
Mozzarella, 121
 Pasta Tubes Baked with Cheese,
  Eggplant, and Tomato Sauce, 134
 Potato Dumplings in a Tomato Sauce
  with Fresh Basil and Melted
  Mozzarella, 126
Mushrooms
 Fresh Hand-Twisted Noodles Topped
  with a Sausage Sauce, 95
 Fresh Pasta Tubes with Porcini
  Mushrooms and Parmesan, 87
 Ham and Ricotta Rolled in a Sheet of
  Pasta and Baked in Béchamel
  Sauce, 90
 Ricotta-Spinach Dumplings Baked
  in a Creamy Porcini Mushroom
  Sauce, 74
 Ridged Tubes with a Meat and Porcini
  Sauce Baked in a Clay Pot, 36
 Stuffed Pasta Tubes Baked in Béchamel
  Sauce with Mushrooms, Tomatoes,
  and Truffles, 39–40
 A Trio of Spinach, Mushroom, and
  Ricotta-Pancetta Dumplings in
  Chicken Stock, 59–60
Mussels
 Fresh Pasta Baked in a Creamy Seafood
  Sauce, 71–72
 Fresh Pasta "Handkerchiefs" with
  Mussels, Beans, and Tomatoes, 140

Mussels, Anchovies, and Tomatoes Tossed with Pasta Strands, 105

Pasta Ribbons, Mussels, Clams, Shrimp, Scallops, and Tomato Sauce Cooked in Parchment, 124

Seafood Baked in a Tomato Sauce with Round Pasta Strands, 69

Naples, 129

Offelle, 12
*Offelle alla Triestina*, 62–63
Potato Ravioli Filled with Spinach and Sausage and Topped with Brown Butter and Sage, 62–63

Olive oil, 17

Olives
Corkscrew Pasta Tossed with a Tuna Sauce, 108
Corkscrew Pasta with a Sauce of Assorted Olives and Fresh Tomatoes, 94
Fat Pasta Tubes in a Fresh Tomato and Olive Sauce, 76

Orecchiette, 15
"Little Ears" of Pasta with Rapini, Anchovies, and Garlic, 143
*Orecchiette con Cime di Rapa*, 143

Pancetta, 112
Fresh Spinach Pasta Ribbons with a Classic Meat Ragù, 85–86
Hollow, Round Pasta Strands in a Classic Sauce of Pancetta and Eggs, 107
Long, Hollow Strands in Tomato and Pancetta Sauce, 112
Ribbed Pasta Tubes in a Creamy Tomato-Vodka Sauce, 53
Small Pasta Shells Topped with a Classic Meat Roll, 139

A Trio of Spinach, Mushroom, and Ricotta-Pancetta Dumplings in Chicken Stock, 59–60

Pansoti, 12
*Pansoti au Preboggion*, 37
Pasta Stuffed with a Wild-Greens Filling and Topped with a Buttermilk Sauce, 37

Pantelleria, 65

Pappardelle, 12, 81
*Pappardelle sull'Anatra*, 97
Wide Pasta Ribbons in a Duck Sauce, 97

Parmigiano-Reggiano, 17, 81
Butternut Squash Pasta Filled with a Butternut Squash, Parmesan, and Walnut Filling, 88
Fresh Pasta Tubes with Porcini Mushrooms and Parmesan, 87

Parsley Pesto, Prawns and Pasta Ribbons with, 131–32

*Pasta al Forno*, 134

*Pasta N'caciata*, 165–66

*Pasticcio di Pesce*, 71–72

Peas
Fresh Pasta Ribbons Baked in a Cream Sauce with Sautéed Ham and Green Peas, 44
Pasta, Ham, Eggs, and Cheese Baked between Eggplant Slices, 165–66

Pecorino, 17, 147
Fat Pasta Tubes with Italian Sausage and Tomatoes, 138
Fresh Pasta Stuffed with an Eggplant-Pecorino Filling, 160
Pasta Ribbons with Fava Beans, Pecorino, and Aged Ricotta, 100
Pasta Tubes Baked with Cheese, Eggplant, and Tomato Sauce, 134
pepato, 168

Penne, 15
Cauliflower, Golden Raisins, and Pine Nuts Tossed with Small Pasta Tubes, 163
A Fiery Tomato Sauce with Small Pasta Tubes, 111

Pasta, Ham, Eggs, and Cheese Baked between Eggplant Slices, 165–66
*Pasta N'caciata*, 165–66
*Penne all'Arrabbiata*, 111
*Penne con Cavolfiore*, 163
Ribbed Pasta Tubes in a Creamy Tomato-Vodka Sauce, 53

Pennette, 15
*Pasta al Forno*, 134
Pasta Tubes Baked with Cheese, Eggplant, and Tomato Sauce, 134
*Pennette con Ricotta Salata*, 135
*Penne Vodka*, 53
Small Pasta Tubes and Lamb Sauce with Aged Ricotta, 135

Pepper, ground, 18

Peppers
peperoncino, 18, 111
Roasted Peppers and Clams with Pasta Strands, 137

Perciatelli, 14
Long, Hollow Strands in Tomato and Pancetta Sauce, 112
*Perciatelli all'Amatriciana*, 112

Perugia, 103

Pesto
Pasta Ribbons Dressed with a Roasted Tomato and Basil Pesto, 167
Pasta Ribbons with Pesto, Green Beans, and Potatoes, 34
Prawns and Pasta Ribbons with Parsley Pesto, 131–32

Pici, 11, 81
Fresh Hand-Twisted Noodles Topped with a Sausage Sauce, 95
*Pici con Salsiccia*, 95

Piemonte, 31, 39–46

Pizzoccheri, 12
*Pizzoccheri della Valtellina*, 48
Savoy Cabbage, Potatoes, Fontina Cheese, and Buckwheat Noodles Baked in a Casserole, 48

Pork
Fresh Spinach Pasta Ribbons with a Classic Meat Ragù, 85–86

Pasta, Ham, Eggs, and Cheese Baked between Eggplant Slices, 165–66
Pasta Stuffed with a Anise-Flavored Filling, 51
Small Pasta Shells Topped with a Classic Meat Roll, 139
Potatoes
  Corkscrew-Shaped Pasta with Tuna, Artichokes, and Tomato Sauce, 114
  Eggplant-Potato Dumplings Topped with a Tomato-Basil Sauce, 73
  Pasta Ribbons with Pesto, Green Beans, and Potatoes, 34
  Potato and Cheese–Filled Ravioli, 153
  Potato Dumplings Baked in a Gorgonzola Sauce, 50
  Potato Dumplings Filled with a Sausage Stuffing and Topped with Tomato Sauce, 43
  Potato Dumplings in a Tomato Sauce with Fresh Basil and Melted Mozzarella, 126
  Potato Dumplings with Calamari and Radicchio, 77
  Potato Ravioli Filled with Spinach and Sausage and Topped with Brown Butter and Sage, 62–63
  Savoy Cabbage, Potatoes, Fontina Cheese, and Buckwheat Noodles Baked in a Casserole, 48
Prawns. *See* Shrimp and prawns
Puglia, 15, 121, 139–43
Punta Sabbioni, 105

Radicchio
  Potato Dumplings with Calamari and Radicchio, 77
  varieties of, 77
Rapini, "Little Ears" of Pasta with Anchovies, Garlic, and, 143
Ravioli, 12. *See also* Cappellacci; Casonsei; Culurgionis; Offelle; Pansoti
  Fresh Pasta Stuffed with an Eggplant-Pecorino Filling, 160

making, 22
Meat and Spinach–Stuffed Pasta with a Red Wine Sauce, 46
*Ravioli alle Melanzane*, 160
*Ravioli al Vino Rosso*, 46
Ricotta, 147
  Beet-Flavored Pasta Stuffed with a Ricotta-Beet Filling Topped with Brown Butter and Poppy Seeds, 66
  Delicate Fresh Crêpes with a Spinach-Ricotta Filling, 93
  Fat Pasta Tubes with Italian Sausage and Tomatoes, 138
  Ham and Ricotta Rolled in a Sheet of Pasta and Baked in Béchamel Sauce, 90
  Pasta Stuffed with a Wild-Greens Filling and Topped with a Buttermilk Sauce, 37
  Ricotta-Spinach Dumplings Baked in a Creamy Porcini Mushroom Sauce, 74
  A Trio of Spinach, Mushroom, and Ricotta-Pancetta Dumplings in Chicken Stock, 59–60
Ricotta salata, 135
  Pasta Ribbons with Fava Beans, Pecorino, and Aged Ricotta, 100
  Pasta Strands Rolled in Eggplant Slices with a Tomato-Basil Sauce, 156
  Small Pasta Tubes and Lamb Sauce with Aged Ricotta, 135
Rigatoni, 15
  Fat Pasta Tubes in a Fresh Tomato and Olive Sauce, 76
  Fat Pasta Tubes with Italian Sausage and Tomatoes, 138
  Pasta, Ham, Eggs, and Cheese Baked between Eggplant Slices, 165–66
*Pasta N'caciata*, 165–66
*Rigatoni alla Calabrese*, 138
*Rigatoni alla Crudaiola*, 76
Rome, 43, 107, 112
*Rotolino di Pasta all' Emiliana*, 90

Saffron and Semolina Dumplings in a Saffron, Sausage, and Lamb Sauce, 155
Salmon, Smoked, Caper, and Brandy Cream Sauce, Bow-Tie Pasta in a, 54
*Salsa di Pomodoro*, 24
Salsicca Calabrese, 138
Salt, sea, 18
Sant'Andrea, 129
Sardegna, 11, 12, 147, 151–55
Sausage, 81, 121
  Fat Pasta Tubes with Italian Sausage and Tomatoes, 138
  Fresh Hand-Twisted Noodles Topped with a Sausage Sauce, 95
  Potato Dumplings Filled with a Sausage Stuffing and Topped with Tomato Sauce, 43
  Potato Ravioli Filled with Spinach and Sausage and Topped with Brown Butter and Sage, 62–63
  Saffron and Semolina Dumplings in a Saffron, Sausage, and Lamb Sauce, 155
  varieties of, 138
Savoy Cabbage, Potatoes, Fontina Cheese, and Buckwheat Noodles Baked in a Casserole, 48
Scallops
  Fresh Pasta Baked in a Creamy Seafood Sauce, 71–72
  Pasta Ribbons, Mussels, Clams, Shrimp, Scallops, and Tomato Sauce Cooked in Parchment, 124
  Seafood Baked in a Tomato Sauce with Round Pasta Strands, 69
Sea urchin
  purchasing and preparing, 158
  Sea Urchin with Pasta Strands, 158
Semolina, 121, 147
Serving, 27
Shrimp and prawns
  Fresh Pasta Baked in a Creamy Seafood Sauce, 71–72

Pasta Ribbons, Mussels, Clams, Shrimp,
    Scallops, and Tomato Sauce Cooked
    in Parchment, 124
Prawns and Pasta Ribbons with Parsley
    Pesto, 131–32
Sautéed Prawns with Capers, Cream,
    and Tomato Sauce over Thin Pasta
    Strands, 65
Seafood Baked in a Tomato Sauce with
    Round Pasta Strands, 69
Thin Pasta Strands with Shrimp and
    Squash Blossoms, 115
Sicilia, 65, 147, 156–68
Siena, 81
Sorrento, 131, 132
Spaghetti, 14
Dried Tuna Roe Shaved into an
    Aromatic Sauce and Tossed with
    Pasta Strands, 152
*Involtini alle Melanzane con Spaghetti*, 156
Mussels, Anchovies, and Tomatoes
    Tossed with Pasta Strands, 105
Pasta Strands Rolled in Eggplant Slices
    with a Tomato-Basil Sauce, 156
Pasta Strands with Black Truffle
    Sauce, 103
Pasta Strands with Garlic, Olive Oil, and
    Dried Red Pepper, 110
Roasted Peppers and Clams with Pasta
    Strands, 137
Sea Urchin with Pasta Strands, 158
*Spaghetti Aglio, Olio e Peperoncino*, 110
*Spaghetti ai Ricci di Mare*, 158
*Spaghetti alla Lucana*, 137
*Spaghetti alla Norcina*, 103
*Spaghetti alle Cozze*, 105
*Spaghetti con la Bottarga*, 152
Spaghettini, 14
A Classic Combination of Thin Pasta
    Strands and Tomato-Basil Sauce, 127
Fresh Crab with Tomatoes and Thin
    Pasta Strands, 98
*Spaghettini al Filetto di Pomodoro*, 127
*Spaghettini al Granchio*, 98
*Spaghettini all'Aragosta*, 151

*Spaghettini con Pesce Spada*, 159
*Spaghettini in Salsa alla Trevisana*, 68
Swordfish, Sautéed Eggplant, and Mint
    with Thin Pasta Strands, 159
Thin Pasta Strands in a Tomato-Anchovy
    Sauce, 68
Thin Pasta Strands with Lobster
    Sauce, 151
Spätzle, 11
making, 23
*Spätzle Crema e Speck*, 56
Spinach Dumplings with a Ham and
    Cream Sauce, 56
Speck, 56
Spinach
Delicate Fresh Crêpes with a Spinach-
    Ricotta Filling, 93
Fresh Spinach Pasta Ribbons with a
    Classic Meat Ragù, 85–86
Meat and Spinach–Stuffed Pasta with a
    Red Wine Sauce, 46
Potato Ravioli Filled with Spinach and
    Sausage and Topped with Brown
    Butter and Sage, 62–63
Ricotta-Spinach Dumplings Baked
    in a Creamy Porcini Mushroom
    Sauce, 74
Spinach Dumplings with a Ham and
    Cream Sauce, 56
A Trio of Spinach, Mushroom, and
    Ricotta-Pancetta Dumplings in
    Chicken Stock, 59–60
Squash
Butternut Squash Pasta Filled with a
    Butternut Squash, Parmesan, and
    Walnut Filling, 88
Sautéed Zucchini and Pasta Ribbons, 168
Thin Pasta Strands with Shrimp and
    Squash Blossoms, 115
*Strangolaprieti alla Sorrentina*, 126
Swordfish, Sautéed Eggplant, and Mint with
    Thin Pasta Strands, 159

Tagliatelle, 11, 81
Fresh Spinach Pasta Ribbons with a
    Classic Meat Ragù, 85–86
Pasta Ribbons with Fava Beans,
    Pecorino, and Aged Ricotta, 100
*Tagliatelle alla Bolognese*, 85–86
*Tagliatelle alle Fave*, 100
Taglierini, 11
Fresh Pasta Ribbons Baked in a Cream
    Sauce with Sautéed Ham and Green
    Peas, 44
*Taglierini Gratinati*, 44
Tagliolini, 11
Fresh Pasta Ribbons in a Butter
    Sauce Topped with Shaved White
    Truffles, 41
Prawns and Pasta Ribbons with Parsley
    Pesto, 131–32
*Tagliolini al Limone*, 131–32
*Tagliolini al Tartufo*, 41
Tomatoes, 81
canned, 18
Cauliflower, Golden Raisins, and Pine
    Nuts Tossed with Small Pasta
    Tubes, 163
A Classic Combination of Thin Pasta
    Strands and Tomato-Basil Sauce, 127
Corkscrew Pasta Tossed with a Tuna
    Sauce, 108
Corkscrew Pasta with a Sauce of
    Assorted Olives and Fresh
    Tomatoes, 94
Corkscrew-Shaped Pasta with Tuna,
    Artichokes, and Tomato Sauce, 114
Eggplant-Potato Dumplings Topped with
    a Tomato-Basil Sauce, 73
Fat Pasta Tubes in a Fresh Tomato and
    Olive Sauce, 76
Fat Pasta Tubes with Italian Sausage and
    Tomatoes, 138
A Fiery Tomato Sauce with Small Pasta
    Tubes, 111
fresh, 18
Fresh Crab with Tomatoes and Thin
    Pasta Strands, 98

Fresh Hand-Twisted Noodles Topped
    with a Sausage Sauce, 95
Fresh Pasta "Handkerchiefs" with
    Mussels, Beans, and Tomatoes, 140
Fresh Pasta Stuffed with an Eggplant-
    Pecorino Filling, 160
Long, Hollow Strands in Tomato and
    Pancetta Sauce, 112
Mussels, Anchovies, and Tomatoes
    Tossed with Pasta Strands, 105
Pasta, Ham, Eggs, and Cheese Baked
    between Eggplant Slices, 165–66
Pasta Ribbons Dressed with a Roasted
    Tomato and Basil Pesto, 167
Pasta Ribbons, Mussels, Clams, Shrimp,
    Scallops, and Tomato Sauce Cooked
    in Parchment, 124
Pasta Shells with Arugula and
    Tomatoes, 116
Pasta Strands Rolled in Eggplant Slices
    with a Tomato-Basil Sauce, 156
Pasta Strands with a Lamb Sauce, 117
Pasta Tubes Baked with Cheese,
    Eggplant, and Tomato Sauce, 134
Potato Dumplings Filled with a Sausage
    Stuffing and Topped with Tomato
    Sauce, 43
Potato Dumplings in a Tomato Sauce
    with Fresh Basil and Melted
    Mozzarella, 126
Potato Dumplings with Calamari and
    Radicchio, 77
Ribbed Pasta Tubes in a Creamy
    Tomato-Vodka Sauce, 53
Saffron and Semolina Dumplings
    in a Saffron, Sausage, and Lamb
    Sauce, 155
Sautéed Prawns with Capers, Cream,
    and Tomato Sauce over Thin Pasta
    Strands, 65
Seafood Baked in a Tomato Sauce with
    Round Pasta Strands, 69
Small Pasta Shells Topped with a Classic
    Meat Roll, 139

Small Pasta Tubes and Lamb Sauce with
    Aged Ricotta, 135
Stuffed Pasta Tubes Baked in Béchamel
    Sauce with Mushrooms, Tomatoes,
    and Truffles, 39–40
Swordfish, Sautéed Eggplant, and Mint
    with Thin Pasta Strands, 159
Thin Pasta Strands in a Tomato-Anchovy
    Sauce, 68
Thin Pasta Strands with Lobster
    Sauce, 151
Tomato Sauce, 24
Wide Pasta Ribbons in a Duck Sauce, 97
Tortiglioni, 15
    Ridged Tubes with a Meat and Porcini
        Sauce Baked in a Clay Pot, 36
    Tortiglioni al Sugo di Carne, 36
Toscana, 11, 12, 17, 81, 93–98
Trápani, 167
Trenette, 14
    Pasta Ribbons with Pesto, Green Beans,
        and Potatoes, 34
    Trenette con Pesto alla Genovese, 34
Trentino–Alto Adige, 11, 31, 54–60
Treviso, 68
Truffles, 18, 31, 81
    Fresh Pasta Ribbons in a Butter
        Sauce Topped with Shaved White
        Truffles, 41
    Pasta Strands with Black Truffle
        Sauce, 103
    preparing, 41
    storing, 41
    Stuffed Pasta Tubes Baked in Béchamel
        Sauce with Mushrooms, Tomatoes,
        and Truffles, 39–40
    Thin Pasta Strands with Lobster
        Sauce, 151
Tuna, 18, 108
    Corkscrew Pasta Tossed with a Tuna
        Sauce, 108
    Corkscrew-Shaped Pasta with Tuna,
        Artichokes, and Tomato Sauce, 114
    Dried Tuna Roe Shaved into an
        Aromatic Sauce and Tossed with
        Pasta Strands, 152

Umbria, 81, 100–103

Val d'Aosta, 31, 39–46
Vallelunga, 165
Veal
    Stuffed Pasta Tubes Baked in Béchamel
        Sauce with Mushrooms, Tomatoes,
        and Truffles, 39–40
Venetian Hotel, 74
Veneto, 12, 14, 31, 66–77
Venezia Giulia. See Friuli–Venezia Giulia
Venice, 68, 74, 76, 105
Vermicelli, 14
    Sautéed Prawns with Capers, Cream,
        and Tomato Sauce over Thin Pasta
        Strands, 65
    Thin Pasta Strands with Fresh Clams
        and Garlic–White Wine Sauce, 129
    Thin Pasta Strands with Shrimp and
        Squash Blossoms, 115
    Vermicelli alla Busara, 65
    Vermicelli alle Vongole, 129
    Vermicelli con Gamberi ai Fiori di Zucchine, 115
Vodka
    Prawns and Pasta Ribbons with Parsley
        Pesto, 131–32
    Ribbed Pasta Tubes in a Creamy
        Tomato-Vodka Sauce, 53

Walnut, Butternut Squash, and Parmesan
    Filling, Butternut Squash Pasta Filled
    with a, 88
Wine, cooking, 18

Zucchini
    Sautéed Zucchini and Pasta Ribbons, 168
    Thin Pasta Strands with Shrimp and
        Squash Blossoms, 115

# TABLE OF EQUIVALENTS

*The exact equivalents in the following tables have been rounded for convenience.*

## LIQUID/DRY MEASURES

| U.S. | Metric |
| --- | --- |
| 1/4 teaspoon | 1.25 milliliters |
| 1/2 teaspoon | 2.5 milliliters |
| 1 teaspoon | 5 milliliters |
| 1 tablespoon (3 teaspoons) | 15 milliliters |
| 1 fluid ounce (2 tablespoons) | 30 milliliters |
| 1/4 cup | 60 milliliters |
| 1/3 cup | 80 milliliters |
| 1/2 cup | 120 milliliters |
| 1 cup | 240 milliliters |
| 1 pint (2 cups) | 480 milliliters |
| 1 quart (4 cups, 32 ounces) | 960 milliliters |
| 1 gallon (4 quarts) | 3.84 liters |
| | |
| 1 ounce (by weight) | 28 grams |
| 1 pound | 454 grams |
| 2.2 pounds | 1 kilogram |

## LENGTH

| U.S. | Metric |
| --- | --- |
| 1/8 inch | 3 millimeters |
| 1/4 inch | 6 millimeters |
| 1/2 inch | 12 millimeters |
| 1 inch | 2.5 centimeters |

## OVEN TEMPERATURE

| Fahrenheit | Celsius | Gas |
| --- | --- | --- |
| 250 | 120 | 1/2 |
| 275 | 140 | 1 |
| 300 | 150 | 2 |
| 325 | 160 | 3 |
| 350 | 180 | 4 |
| 375 | 190 | 5 |
| 400 | 200 | 6 |
| 425 | 220 | 7 |
| 450 | 230 | 8 |
| 475 | 240 | 9 |
| 500 | 260 | 10 |